My Life s journey

My Life's Journey

Doreen Ramus

Library and Archives Canada Cataloguing in Publication

Ramus, Doreen, author
    My life's journey / Doreen Ramus.

    1. Ramus, Doreen. 2. Nurses--Canada--Biography.
3. British--Canada--Biography. 4. Immigrants--Canada--
Biography. I. Title.

RT37.R34A3 2016   610.73092   C2016-903676-6

ISBN 978-1533327802

Cover image by Doreen Ramus

Author image by Sarah Ramus

Design and layout by Margreet Dietz

Contents

With love to my children,
Helen, Bruce and Sarah

And my grandchildren,
Michael, Daniel, Lisa, Shannon, Mitchell and Sam

Life is either a daring adventure, or nothing. To keep our faces toward change and behave like free spirits in the presence of fate is strength undefeatable.

Helen Keller

My Tree

The play was *Charley's Aunt*. We needed a small tree to create a garden scene. A twig-like copper beech tree was bought. *Charley's Aunt* closed. I took the "tree" home and planted it outside the window of my son's basement bedroom.

Forty years flew by.

Now my beech tree has grown above the roof of my two-story home, passing by my own bedroom window. I gaze on it with awe and love each morning as I wrench myself out of bed.

In winter the bare branches reach out to the short-lived light. Blue Jays perch and add to the alarm bells of the morning. Squirrels scuttle rapidly from branch to branch lest there be some morsel to digest.

Spring arrives and slowly fattening buds appear on those branches, filling out in size daily until—oh joy—a green leaf bursts forth, multiplying daily until the whole tree is clothed in verdant foliage.

As summer approaches, the longer days of light infiltrate the leaves, gradually turning them, as if tanned by the sun, to a deep, shiny brown.

Autumn follows and slowly the leaves change again to a golden copper, filling my room with light. It is the one burst of remembrance and I marvel at all the transitions.

As the winds blow and the rains and snow of winter beat upon the tree, it is as if the branches are trying to keep those brilliant leaves from falling. But no, they too must drop, layering the earth in gold.

And we are back to bare branches again, a time for reflection and a hope for spring.

Arrival

On July 28th, 1926, around 4.50am, Father was standing on the steps of our old, rather ugly, vicarage in Milton Lilbourne, Wilts, England. Dr. Gedge had been summoned, as a birth was imminent. As Father looked out on that ever-brightening dawn in the summer sky, he spotted an owl perched on the top of the flagpole that stood tall on our front lawn. Suddenly, from inside the house, they both heard the cry of a newborn. The owl flew away. I had arrived!

MILTON VICARAGE — 'X' WHERE I WAS BORN

My home was a haven of security. My mother, large and enveloping, was ever present during those early years. I hated her out of my sight. My father, a thin man dressed always in the garb of a priest—black with a wide, white dog collar—was more foreboding. He was stern, yet never scolded me in anyway. I stood in awe of him and as I got older he really scared me. I could not be in a room alone with him and really I have no reason why. He always kept me safe.

The other security in my life in those early years was Maude, the deaf and orphaned "maid" who had been with my parents already eight years. Small with a sallow complexion, glasses and rather greasy hair always cut short, Maude was a pillar of strength and security.

Maude's domain was the kitchen. It must be hard for the modern generation to understand this mode of living. In my parents' homes it had been the norm to have maids to deal with all the home chores—both my parents had grown up with this. Father was now a vicar and Mother was expected to help him in much of his work in the village and with many of the village functions. It was expected of Mother to visit the village people, as did Father. We lived in a huge house, which was loaned to us from the diocese. We had no choice as to finding or living in a smaller house. This was it and it was expected of my parents to go along.

The house consisted of a huge hallway downstairs, a study for Father, a large dining room (miles from the kitchen), a sitting room and in the nether regions a room where the washing up was done, a kitchen with a walk-in larder, and another outer room for laundry and boot cleaning. Upstairs (there were both front and back stairs) were four bedrooms, a bathroom, a "john" and a huge room we called the nursery. In the attic were two more rooms, one a bedroom and the other a box room where all the suitcases and trunks were stored.

Maude was the hub around which all this operated. Perhaps today she might be equated to a live-in babysitter, but she was far more than that. She cleaned, scrubbed, washed, cooked all meals—on a coal stove that had to be cleaned and lit daily, stated what needed to be bought for all this, told the gardener what veggies she wanted for that day, dealt with cats forever having kittens in her kitchen cupboards, cleaned the fireplaces and laid them for the next fire, which was daily in wintertime, and looked after all of us.

My sister Anne was ten years older than me and away at school in term time, as were my brothers Martin, six years older, and Bryan, four years older. During the holidays we were all at home and, I am sure, needed a lot of attention.

BRYAN ANNE
WITH NEBORN DOREEN

Maude's day would start before 6am by first lighting the kitchen stove, by lamplight as there was no electricity, in order to boil the kettle for my parents' early morning tea, which she took to them, and Father's shaving water. Next Maude swept the stairs with brush and dustpan, dealt with fireplaces and readied the dining room for breakfast, which she then cooked. There was always a cooked breakfast: eggs and bacon, sausages, spaghetti tossed in bacon fat, or fish of some sort. Then Maude and Mother would go into the larder and discuss what would be on the menu that day, while Father cleaned the tea and coffee pots in the washing-up room. Don't ask me why this was his ritual. It was forever thus. Mother and Maude would repair to the bedrooms and make all beds, which should have been stripped to air. Mother, often helped by one of us, would do the breakfast washing up.

Needless to say, it was Maude's job to clean the bedrooms and bathroom, nursery and kitchen areas, and this was done daily. She often spent time with us in the nursery or took us out for a walk, often with the purpose of buying cookies for the household at some remote place through the fields. We all loved those safaris. She was never impatient with us, never said, "I'm too busy for you today," never got mad at us. Maude was always there for us. When we needed comfort, we only had to find Maude in her warm kitchen and it all just swept over us.

ON HOLIDAY
MAUDE MARTIN. BRYAN DOREEN

My parents were busy people, with the life of our village and other villages in Father's charge. We didn't have a car so they went everywhere on foot or by bike. They too were always there for us in a miraculous sort of way.

Meals were at a designated time. It was expected of all of us to be present and to stand behind our chairs before Father would say grace. Yes, it was a disciplined household. We usually cleared

6

away our meals by taking everything out to the washing up room. Maude of course ate her meals in the kitchen.

Coffee and cookies were served at 11am and lunch was usually a substantial meal with a pudding of sorts served at 1pm. Tea came next at 4pm and this was a sit down affair in the dining room. We could have bread and butter first, then a piece with jam. A piece of yesterday's cake was then allowed before we were able to partake of today's. Think of the cooking that all this entailed!

Maude could have been termed a slave, but she was a saint and always appeared happy with all of us. She wore a pink dress with a bibbed apron in the mornings and changed into a black dress with a frilly white apron and frilly cap after lunch. Always black shoes and thick stockings.

Supper was served at 7.30pm with a big green oil lamp set in the middle of the table. In my early years I was not present at this meal, but safely tucked up in bed for the night, having had a little supper in the nursery. Tea and cookies were served at 9pm before Maude could finally go to bed after filling all hot water bottles.

When I was five, I went to the village school, usually taken by Muriel and Freddy who lived next door. I was a bit scared of it all especially the two sisters who taught there. The Miss Pickens were pretty stern women and I really don't think I learnt much except to talk like the other village kids—with a strong Wiltshire accent. This was really my downfall. When my sister and brothers came home from boarding school for the holidays they teased me unmercifully. I had no idea what made them laugh at me so much.

I always looked forward to my siblings coming home and Father would hang all the church flags out, with one on the flagpole, to welcome them. It was exciting at first and we all had fun riding bikes round our lovely big garden. One particular path, known as the black hill, descended into the garage area. It was frightening to go down, but I always felt I had to keep up with the others and usually either fell off or crashed into a wall at the bottom.

Village Life

In school I sat next to Frances Wells. We shared a double desk with inkwells. I used to watch Frances write with her pen dipped in the ink and marvel. I could never get my writing to shine like that! We learned to knit for which I have always been grateful. It was not easy at first. One day I was knitting a square with very thick string-like orange yarn when I seemed to get a knot in it. I was far too scared to ask for help, so I continued, pretending to knit. When the class was over, I stuffed my knitting in my pocket and took it home to Maude who dealt with it in her usual calm way.

Of course Sunday was church day. I went to the 11am service and watched Father in his long black cassock with the white nightie-looking shirt over the top. It was a sombre affair except for the hymns, which Mother seemed to lead. I also went to Sunday school of course and liked the stamps that I had to stick in my book. Whatever I may have learnt from all this was purely by osmosis I believe.

One of my favourite pastimes was washing the rubbish bin lids. Situated outside our back door under a huge yew tree, the bins caught splats of the red berries together with white bird droppings. Maude would give me an old jam jar filled with water and an old rag. I spent many an hour washing the lids. All so satisfying.

Across the road—which was really only a very narrow paved country road, from our house—was King Hall. It had impressive gates and a circular driveway up to the impressive front door of the huge house set in a beautiful walled garden. The Butlers lived here. Mr. Butler, a quiet gentleman farmer, and his wife had two daughters. Cecil, the youngest, was perhaps six years older than me but she became my very first friend. We played for hours in the woods in their garden and had many secret hiding spots to retreat to. Often we would go up into the lofts of the horse barns where there was always hay to roll around in and often kittens to play with. Sometimes I was allowed inside the house to play in the schoolroom, which again was fun. They seemed to have so many interesting cupboards.

Lo, their nanny, was really formidable. She was always dressed in black and I was scared of her.

Mrs. Butler was very aristocratic and to be invited to stay for tea was rather scary, too. Mr. Butler sat at one end, always very quiet with a wonderful twinkle in his eyes. Mrs. Butler, seated at the other end of the table that seemed a mile long, served out the tea, filling the teapot by a brass kettle that stood on a stand by her side. It fascinated me. I was in awe of the whole household, but I loved going there.

Sometimes on a Saturday the Hunt would gather at King Hall before setting off. This was a magnificent sight. Many beautiful horses would be led onto the driveway. Groomsmen would help the huntsmen, dressed in their traditional red coats, black caps and white jodhpurs, up onto their steeds. Mrs. Butler, like most of the other ladies, would be in black, with a long black skirt, and she would ride sidesaddle—often issuing out many orders to the servants. The hounds would be excitedly jumping about, itching to get going, but first a servant would come out and offer drinks, usually whisky, to the riders from a silver tray. As I stood by Father one day watching all this excitement, I was asked what I would like to drink. Having heard Father state his preference, I too asked for whisky! This of course caused guffaws of laughter. I was never quite sure why.

On Christmas Eve we were always invited to King Hall to witness the Christmas tree. All the servants including Maude were present around the tree and we watched the handing out of gifts to all and sundry. It was awe-inspiring and my only recollection of a tree in my youth.

Mother was a great person for getting up entertainment for the village or the church. When I was quite small I had to be Goldilocks and act on the village stage known as the Memorial Hall. I can still see those bare floorboards. I am sure my head was always down, I was so shy. On the same night Mother got on stage and acted out some nursery rhyme where someone had to cut her petticoats. I was terrified and, for the first and only time in my life, sought refuge in Father's arms.

One of the walks Maude took us on led towards the cemetery just past our walled garden. In a corner by the wall was a yew tree and here lived my imaginary rabbit. Every time we went on this walk I took it grass to eat. At the back of the garden were all the grass clippings from the lawn mower—a huge pile of them and one could pretend to put eggs in them like a nest. To put my hand in was fascinating for, no matter how cold it was outside, there was always warmth in amongst those clippings.

The Memorial Hall was close to this area and when there was a meeting going on there we would crawl underneath the Hall and listen to them singing "Jerusalem," always led confidently by Mother.

Towards the end of our time in Milton, Father purchased a huge Austin 12. It seemed massive and the minute I got in, it just lulled me to sleep, often on Mother's lap. When it was parked outside the front door one day, ready to take off down the driveway, I hopped in and released the brake. Luckily I hopped out again to watch it sliding down the hill to the gate. I can't remember any fury or damage, which makes me realize what a calm, peaceful and loving family I lived in. Nevertheless, I learnt my lesson.

School Years

In 1935 we moved to the south of Wiltshire to a small village called Barford St. Martin, six miles from Salisbury. Perhaps this was the happiest time of my growing up—apart from school life. I was sent to Godolphin School for girls as a daygirl, catching a bus every morning to Salisbury and then walking up a monumental hill to the forbidding school at the top. On Mondays another village family, whose son went as a weekly boarder to Salisbury Cathedral School, took me. This, in a sense, was a reprieve from that hill, but I had to ride in the back of their open car, known as the "dickie". We wore straw boaters and I never had the sense to remove it while blowing along in the car. It was a battle. To come home from school I had to catch a certain bus from the town, which cost me three pennies. If I missed it I panicked. The lavatories in the school looked like the public ones where for which you needed a penny to use them. I only had three pennies for the bus so it was a long time before I caught on that these didn't need pennies. It was also a long day!

When I first started at Godolphin, I was asked where I came from. I suppose I noticed that their accent was akin to my parents. To speak the Queen's English was a mark of breeding and education. An accent or dialect was a sign that you came from a lower class of people (the good old British class distinction era).

Oi cum fram Baarford snt Maarten, thaats wurr oi cum frum.

Eowa, and wot does yaw Fathuh doo?

Moi faaterrs a paarsen, thaats wot e is.

My Wiltshire accent was my downfall: I was laughed at and put down at every turn. I hated it. I was good at nothing and hated games and gym. It all seemed so pointless. I couldn't wait to get out and head home every day. Eventually I learnt to speak as they did, which in fact I am grateful for.

Another episode that went against me was with my teeth. Though my parents had insisted on the very best dentist, somehow he missed an abscess forming in my front tooth. This then had to come out and a different dentist was chosen. He then found that the infection had spread to two other teeth in the front; so all three teeth were gone. A plate was made and it seemed every lunch hour I had to walk into town for "a fitting". Eventually I had new front teeth, which seemed like a bunch of plum stones in my mouth and of course made me look different.

Games Excuse

At this time too, I had noticed a pad of paper on the notice board that was headed "games excuse" and listed several names underneath. The list was renewed every day. What a great idea. If I didn't have to play games after school, I could get the early bus home. I added my name. The games prefect then accosted me, having noticed my name for two weeks straight, and asked me if my mother knew. What on earth did it have to do with my mother? When I did consult Mother she told me that sometimes you did not need to play games, usually for about five days a month. Fair enough. Every month I made sure that my name went down from a Monday to a Friday! I guess I finally caught on when we were on holiday by the sea and Anne had promised to teach me how to swim. Her promise failed. I was devastated. Mother then explained all about the birds, bees and chickens. To this day I am not sure about the chickens.

BARFORD RECTORY

The Parsonage

Home was blessedly different. The house was huge, shaped like a Z. It had been built in the 13th century for monks and the kitchen had been used as their refectory—dining hall. The walls were four feet thick in parts and we all felt that many ghosts inhabited the house. It had the usual huge dining room, sitting room and hallway. Beyond the kitchen, with its enormous kitchen table, were several scullery-type rooms and another room my parents made into a chapel. Right at the end of all these outer rooms was a washroom, complete with "copper," a huge concrete bowl with a small firebox underneath it. Every Monday, Isabel, the gardener's wife, poured water into this vast copper, lit the fire and spent the whole day washing clothes. It was a major production. Also in this room was a hand pump that was used to pump water up from a well to a vast tank at the top of the back stairs for use throughout the house. This was usually done by Tom, the gardener, twice a day.

Upstairs there were five bedrooms as well as a study and dressing room for Father. Above all this were two separate attics. One had four rooms in it where my brothers had their bedroom, sitting room, train room and studio. The other attic had two rooms, one a bedroom and the other the box room. There was a bathroom at one end of the bedroom floor and a john at the other. A small coke stove in the kitchen heated water, while Maude cooked on a coal stove. The house was not centrally heated of course, so there were the usual fires in the rooms in winter. The only really warm room was the kitchen! We did at least have electricity.

I think I can safely say that we all loved this house with its huge garden, tennis court and space. The village was delightful with such friendly people. Anne, by this time, was heading away to study Domestic Science in London. Both boys were still at boarding school, though Martin was soon to go to a private school in Salisbury for a short while, before going on to art school.

Bus Service

Transportation to and from Salisbury was really a new thing for me. Probably the only time I had been on a tour bus was to go with the Sunday school and my parents on an outing to the sea once a year. Now busses were a daily occurrence.

At first the village bus was run by two brothers. The Viney brothers were great people. The one who drove had only one leg and the one who took the money and gave out the tickets had only one arm. They managed brilliantly and were always so cheerful. I felt completely safe with them and they would sometimes wait for me if I was late coming down from school.

Soon a bigger outfit took over the bus line, which initially seemed a bit impersonal after the Vineys. However, one learns and soon I came to know Charlie, the bus conductor. He had the kindest disposition and face. As long as Charlie was there, all would be well. Charlie was in my life for a long time and I guess when my hormones started to flutter I fell in love with him and asked him if he would please wait for me so that I could marry him! He just gave me his great smile and said, "I'll try."

I learnt later to my sorrow that of course he was already married.

Friends

Being a parson—or rector, as Father was known—in a village was like being in charge of it. Father was someone who was revered and looked up to. Because of this status, none of us were allowed to make friends of the village people as this would show favouritism. Perhaps this was not so bad for my brothers and sister as they were away at school, but for me it was hard. I was pretty lonely and even snuck out one day and joined the village boys outside our house playing soccer. That was a no-no.

At the bottom of our garden lived a family who had a girl my age. Finally my parents consented for us to be friends. Gwen and I had so much fun together. She was allowed to come to the rectory to play and we cycled and camped together. We were always the best of friends. She went to a different school in Salisbury, which I envied, but we rode on the same bus. Her home was as strict as mine and sometimes when I went to call for her she had "other things" to do and was not allowed out, which often left me crushed. Gwen had two brothers and a sister. They lived in a tiny house. Perhaps her parents didn't want her to become too familiar with the way my family lived. It made no difference to me. People just lived the way they lived and that was that!

I can't ever remember Father having a friend. Mother had a friend, Mrs. Hales, who lived a good fifteen miles by bus from us. Mother went to visit her and Mrs. Hales came to tea with us on alternate Thursday afternoons. I got the impression that Father was not too happy about this liaison.

Life at home during this period of my life was idyllic. There was always a lot going on. I was in the church choir, which was led by Father. Mother directed plays, which I took part in. When King George VI was crowned, Mother along with the whole village put on a huge supper in a farmer's barn for everyone to celebrate. People came and went. One summer we had two boys, one from

France and one from the Netherlands, to stay for about three weeks. It was fun. Both my brothers were home too.

At one time I developed mononucleosis and had a collapsed lung, so couldn't go to school for about three months. Oh joy! Anne took over my schoolwork then, which was a bit scary. She taught me every morning and I probably learnt more than I ever did at school! During the summer holidays we usually went on holiday to the coast in the south of England. It was not much of a holiday for Father as we usually exchanged with a parson in that area. It was known as "house for duty". We always enjoyed these breaks. Maude usually came along with us, unless she was snatching a break with her friend Florry, as Maude had no family of her own—she grew up in an orphanage. We really couldn't imagine this. Occasionally I was sent to Broadstone in Dorset where my uncle and aunt, the Chataways, lived with their two young sons, Christopher and Michael, and their baby daughter, Susan. I liked going there if only I hadn't been so homesick all the time. They were all so good to me and tried so hard to make me happy. (To this day, Christopher Chataway remains one of my best friends.) But I was such a homebody and missed it all too much.

Mother became a real nurse in the village and often people would come to her for advice and treatment. It was quite common to see some unfortunate person with a ghastly-infected finger or toe sitting in Maude's kitchen twice a day soaking the offending part in a pudding basin full of near boiling water. Then Mother would plank a great hot wedge of antiphlogistine on it to "draw the poison out". Everyone thought Mother was wonderful and she loved it. If you had a sty on your eye, you sat with the good old basin of boiling water and a wooden spoon with boric acid lint tied round it, dipped it in the water and held it to your eye until the sty burst and there was relief and satisfaction all round. One day one of the farmers was out with his gun, tripped and shot some toes off. They sent for Mother and she wrapped up the toes with the foot and packed him off to hospital. I think they did save the toes. Living close to the crossroads of two major roads meant many accidents to which Mother was always called.

Sundays

Sundays were very different in our house—though I never thought so at the time. After I was confirmed, it was expected of me to attend Holy Communion at least once a month. This was at 8am. Breakfast came next, and then I went back to church to robe for the choir at 11am. This lasted till 12.30pm. Once a month Father had an additional communion service after this. We were not allowed to speak to him until after the second service, even though we robed in the same vestry. Father had his breakfast alone in his study on these occasions. After all these morning rituals were over, the whole family (if at home) would then walk round the garden, inspecting fruit, flowers and vegetables. I really enjoyed this. It felt so relaxing somehow. Maude had then prepared Sunday lunch; roast beef and Yorkshires and pudding! Always so good and soporific.

However, next came Sunday school and the dining room was prepared for this. The table was pushed to one side. Chairs were brought down from all over the house and laid out in rows. Father took a short service followed by a hymn and then the kids, including me, all scattered to different rooms according to their ages. They took their chairs with them. My parents and one other adult taught the classes till around 3.30pm, when all the chairs had to be returned. Teatime, which we all attended, at 4pm had been laid ready by Maude before she took off for her "half day." Back to church for 6pm evensong and home again around 7.30pm. Maude had prepared soup and sandwiches for supper, all of which I disliked, mainly because the kitchen itself was so desolate without her presence. Those were Sundays in the Blyth household.

Every morning after breakfast, if I was not at school, Maude would be called from the kitchen and we all sank to our knees in the dining room, usually leaning on one of the cane bottom seats of a chair while Father said morning prayers. This was a ritual that went on regardless of any overnight visitors we may have had, which sometimes could be embarrassing. George, our beloved wire-haired fox terrier, would at this time be allowed into the dining room. He sat on a very wide windowsill and watched the birds outside. If you could inch your way on your knees close enough to him, you could whisper, "Birdies." George would get all excited and bark! This just made a slight deviation from the norm.

Christmas

Christmas was another ritual that has always stood out in my mind. The morning of Christmas Eve was spent decorating the church with holly and evergreen boughs and any flowers that might have been donated. (There were never poinsettias). After lunch there would be a huge dustsheet on our hall floor, full of evergreens to decorate our own house. This we all did listening to the radio broadcast of King's College Choir of Cambridge singing the Festival of Nine Lessons and Carols. It was a tradition and to this day that music and those voices take me right back.

Until I was about fourteen, Christmas Day dawned for me with my stocking at the end of my bed. Father Christmas had not let me down. One Christmas, Martin told me that he had seen Father Christmas and that he had even picked up his handkerchief from the floor. I was in awe! There was the usual church ritual all morning and after Christmas dinner we waited till Maude had washed up and then we all gathered in the sitting room to open presents. Our gifts were piled on individual chairs, no fancy wrapping paper, mostly just good old brown paper. I always hung back so that I would have gifts to open after everyone else had finished. I then would try and write my thank-you notes right away so that I could gloat over the others who were always being reminded to write theirs.

We passed the rest of the day reading new books, playing new board games, and with Mother and Father at the piano, all of us trying to make ourselves heard above Mother's strong singing voice. On New Year's Eve, the church bell ringers would ring out the old year and at midnight ring in the new one, followed by a supper for them all at the rectory. That was fun.

The War Years

It was 1939, the start of the war years. These for me could fill a book but I will try and condense them. I was thirteen, a pretty impressionable age. A lot of people showed sympathy for us during those years in England. I think I can look back on them as an experience that made me stronger.

My parents, Bryan and I were on holiday at the coast when the news came through that the UK and France had declared war on Germany. We returned immediately to the village. Martin had just finished a year at art school and was about to continue. Anne was working as a legal secretary in Salisbury and lived at home, when she wasn't gadding about. Bryan and I were still at school. Bryan returned to his boarding school in the southwest of England. Needless to say Martin went straight into the army. Anne volunteered as an ambulance driver in Salisbury and, when on call, spent the night in a shelter there.

England went into high gear and was really mobilized to the hilt. Mother soon got swept up into the swing. She organized all the teenagers—boys and girls alike—into taking first aid courses from St. John Ambulance. We all wore uniforms and had to pass exams. As many women as Mother could coerce were also taught first aid by St. John Ambulance. Our little chapel in the house was turned into a first aid post, with very conceivable bit of first aid. Mother thought of everything. The men of the village who were not in the forces were mobilized too. Some, including Father, were trained as Air Raid Wardens and wore boiler suits and hard hats. Father looked so funny in his, with his ever-present dog collar. Other men volunteered as the Home Guard. These were put on a roster of about four men per night who went up onto the downs overlooking the village from a shepherd's hut supposedly watching for parachutists or incendiary bombs. Gwen and I visited them sometimes. They seemed dedicated but quite happy.

Next came the gas masks! These were issued to everyone and had to be carried at all times. I suppose you could equate the size of these things to a modern movie camera. They were a pain in the neck to carry around even though they did have a shoulder strap. Then we all had to be re-vaccinated against smallpox. This seemed a bit irrelevant.

Then came evacuees. These were mostly children from towns that were thought to be danger zones for bomb attacks. The village people took them into their homes unquestionably. Some of the evacuees were not easy to deal with and not used to village life— something else for my parents to smooth over.

Blackout was put into effect immediately after war was declared. There were no streetlights of any kind. Car lights were shaded and kept to a minimum of brightness. All windows in buildings had to be completely blacked out. The job of the air raid warden was to go round making sure there was not even a chink of light showing. Our house was no exception and with that many rooms it was quite a nightmare. Our only saving grace was the fact that most windows had been equipped with wooden shutters indoors. Even so, these were old and warped so stripping had to be fixed to them to eliminate any light getting through. Maude's kitchen window had to have special blinds made and all windows had to have masking tape crisscrossed all over them to prevent glass shattering.

1940 saw the capitulation of our forces in Europe. We knew Martin had gone to France and hardly dared think about what had happened to him. One night the phone rang. Anne answered it.

"Has the rector got any petrol? I will be in Wilton market place," a male voice at the other end asked.

Wilton was three miles away. Father at once thought it was one of the villagers who had missed a bus. Petrol was rationed, but he had enough to get there and back. He and Mother took off and were gone far too long. Eventually they came in the back door accompanied by Martin in a uniform that was white from the chest down. We stared. So many questions.

The white was salt from wading into the sea at Dunkirk carrying the wounded onto the millions of little rescue ships. Eventually Martin too had hopped aboard. The reason that it took Mother and Father so long was that they had been stopped as their car lights were too bright!

I shall never forget that night. Maude sat Martin down at the kitchen table and quickly boiled up the one egg that was our ration for the week and spread him some bread and precious butter. He was alive. He was home. Nothing else mattered. Anne, Mother and Father and I just stared at him, unable to believe our eyes. Eventually we all went to bed but not before Maude told Martin, "Put your washing out." The ever-thoughtful, practical Maude.

Later the next day, as we started to really understand the severity of what was happening to our world, Maude took Martin aside. "Mr. Martin, when did you last change your underwear? I have always told you to change on a Monday and this underwear has *not* been changed for several Mondays." Things must be put into perspective. War or no war!

MARTIN AND MAUDE

I hated having to go to school the following day. I just didn't want to lose sight of him again. However I had to go and Martin had a lot of rehabilitating to do.

Whenever Martin left the house to go back off leave, he would never want us to say goodbye. He asked us to stay in the sitting room where he would put on a record of Edward Elgar's *Enigma Variations*. When the record was over, he would have left. It was always the most painful time for me but, as I look back, how much more painful it must have been for him and my parents. One time Father snuck out. Martin was heading for the war in North Africa. I had pleaded with Mother not to let Martin go, thinking that she was invincible. Father stood at the front door. Neither of them knew what to say lest their emotions got the better of them.

Finally Father spoke. "You know, Martin; you are going to be as bald as me when you are forty."

Martin left, enraged. Couldn't Father have said, "Good luck"?

It wasn't till Martin was on the troop ship heading for North Africa that he realized Father knew he was going to *live* till he was forty anyway!

War really heated up then. One night Mother and I were sleeping in the same room, a practice she often did when I was ill, when we heard an aircraft droning round and round. Suddenly a train chuffed past our house through the open cutting and over the bridge. Its firebox lit up the sky. Then the scream of bombs descending pierced the night. Mother threw herself on top of me as six terrifying thuds rocked the house. Bryan came down from the attic with his makeshift flashlight—a candle in a jam jar. Yes we were both fine. Father then came and told Anne to get on her bike and check the village in case anyone was injured or needed help. This of course she did and found that the bombs had landed in the water meadows, just missing the village. A few windows were broken but luckily no one was injured. We considered ourselves lucky but were never complacent.

Rationing, of course, was in full swing. Meat, butter, tea, sugar, eggs, petrol, clothes and shoes were the things I remember. How Mother and Maude were able to provide the meals they did I shall never know. Once a week the fishmonger would send a package on the bus from Salisbury. It usually contained fish, sometimes a rabbit or chicken. This was a godsend. Our garden provided us with plenty of fruit and vegetables.

By 1941 Bryan had left school and went straight into the army in the Signal Corps and was sent to Egypt where he remained for the rest of the war. Anne started working as a secretary at the Headquarters of the Southern Command that was housed in a beautiful old stately house in Wilton. She and her friend, Connie, were really having a great time. They volunteered on Saturdays to help at the forces canteens in Salisbury as a lot of army and air force were stationed near the town. Anne and Connie always seemed to have a stream of eligible young army officers in tow and were never at a loss for entertainment. This made me envious. They seemed to have so much fun. I volunteered eventually, but I was so shy that all I could do was make sandwiches in the kitchen!

School for me was still the eternal grind. The only bright spot was when the sirens went and we all had to go to our designated shelters. Final exams were looming and so much seemed to be expected of me. I was certainly no scholar, always at the bottom of every exam result list and always trying to get out of wretched "games".

Home was best. Anne became engaged to Bill Walker who, I could tell, was not exactly my parents' choice. He was soon posted to India. Mother then suggested to Anne that she apply to go overseas with St John Ambulance as an occupational therapist. Anne was accepted and off she went on a troop ship to North Africa. It was on this ship that she met her good friend Hazel, who was a physiotherapist, and also an officer named Rodney Vaughan. Anne worked in the 97th British field hospital and managed to meet up with Martin. On their time off they were invited to the home of Mme. Miglanico who was extremely kind to them. On hearing that Mme. Miglanico's nephew, Andre Figuiere, was about to go to England to train as a Free French Parachutist, my sister gave our address and told her to be sure to tell Andre to visit our parents so that they could reciprocate her kindness.

MOTHER — IN CHARGE
OF ALL EMERGENCIES

Disaster Scenarios

Meanwhile Mother was in her element—or was it an escape from worrying about her three children far away in a wretched war? What was the future going to hold for them, all in the prime of their lives?

Mother threw herself into first aid practices. She set the scenes and everyone had to participate. She found old toothbrushes, broke off the handles and set them in red sealing wax. These then denoted broken bones. Volunteers (or were they really?) were then placed all around the village with these horrid looking things attached to various parts of their bodies. The first aid "battalion" would be sent out to find and treat them, sending for stretchers and help where needed. Fires were imagined and the stirrup pump brigade was forced into action with their pumps and buckets. Nothing was left to chance! It really drew the whole village together and everyone loved it. Except perhaps Father who, during one of these exercises, had lain in a drain for several hours with toothbrush handles sticking out all over him. Eventually the organist found him and fluttered over him. It was all too much. Father took one look at her and said, "Don't worry about me, Miss Lewis, I've been dead quite a long time."

Mother was not pleased. That was *not* in her plan.

During these escapades Maude kept us all on an even keel; always the backup for everything, always in her kitchen when I came home from school, ready to listen and give such practical and sane advice. With most of the family gone, our huge house was pretty empty so my parents offered to take in two families who were in a danger zone on the coast. They were housed in the attic where my brothers had their rooms. The women were sisters and each had a preschool child. One of them was expecting another. They cooked in Maude's kitchen on a paraffin three-burner stove. They were really no trouble, but I'm sure Maude found them a bit much. Their children often got in Maude's way, but she never complained. They washed all their nappies at Maude's sink and dried them round the fire upstairs. Father often remarked on the delightful odour wafting down to his study. The district nurse safely delivered the baby in the bedroom of the attic. I thought that quite the bonus.

I loved children and it was suggested to me that I might like to help out a woman who had a baby, was expecting another and was not in very good health. So every Saturday I would collect Christopher in an old pram and bring him through the village to our house. Sometimes he slept or I would play with him. I loved it all. Next came Shirley. I bundled Christopher and Shirley in the pram. After this came Martin, who was very ill with whooping cough. He survived and was also put in the pram. Then it was Gordon I think. By that time, Christopher could walk. They were great kids and I loved them all.

When all this came to an end I spent my Saturdays delivering mail to the two small communities up in Grovely Woods. This was about three miles away, so I rode my bike, first to a couple of houses then along through the woods on a cart track to a bigger community of about six houses. They were always so pleased to see me. I would pick up their letters to be mailed in Barford. A little further along was an old farmhouse where two brothers and their sister ran a dairy farm. Here I would stop and drink a lovely fresh warm glass of milk. It was a fascinating place and seemed so far from civilization *and* from the real world. One of the brothers was mentally impaired; they all cared so much for each other and were so kind to me. Getting back to the post office I would be given a shilling. I felt pretty proud of that.

I did have a sort of a boyfriend during these times. Before the war my parents were persuaded to buy pop from a delivery truck. I am sure this went against all my parents' principles but they actually enjoyed it too. Jack Budgell delivered it and he was rather good looking with very nice false teeth that really lit up his face when he smiled. When war broke out, Jack became a chauffeur for some bigwig in the air force. He looked even more attractive in air force blue uniform. So there was no more pop, but he wrote long letters to me all about his life in the forces. When he was on leave, he visited me at our house. I would buy cigarettes for him in between his visits (with my shilling that I earned every week!). He would spend a morning with me and once we walked to Wilton through Grovely Woods. There was nothing sexual about our relationship. He really was much older than me and when I look back I wonder what the attraction was for him? Must have just been the cigarettes, I guess, but he always wrote such great letters. I was excited to get them and reply. I later learnt that he was married which I guess cooled the relationship.

Whenever the army had manoeuvres near us, Mother would always offer them cups of tea. This worried Maude as we were so closely rationed, but Mother was convinced that we would always have enough—and we did. People would share a lot of food with each other. One early morning Mother heard our front gate click, followed by footsteps coming up the path to the front door. She looked out to see a soldier who asked if we had a room with a telephone in it. The only one was my parents' bedroom, and it was 5am. Mother bundled my rather reluctant father out of bed and invited the soldier in. A whole platoon of men then entered our house, with a brigadier and officers taking over the bedroom as their HQ. Poor Maude, who was deaf, knocked on my parents' door at the usual early morning teatime and found rather a different sight than she had expected. They stayed all day on manoeuvres, but I had to go to school.

Another of Mother's activities was to organize village dances. These were primarily to raise money for "comforts for the troops". Two blind pianists walked from Wilton to perform at these dances. They were fabulous; one of them played the drums sometimes too, and the rhythm they kept up was amazing. One man had no eyes at all and his dark glasses would slip down his nose as he played with such energy and gusto. Those empty sockets absolutely fascinated me.

A lot of American troops by this time were stationed near Barford, and locals used to describe them as "over-fed, over-sexed and over here." They would come to the dances, too. One night a dozen eggs that had been donated by a farmer was raffled. Mother picked out the winning ticket. It belonged to an American who proceeded to crack each egg one by one, swallowing them raw and whole. Mother quickly and diplomatically escorted him out the door before he was lynched. Unfortunately these troops did not make a very good impression on us.

Salisbury itself was not bombed, mercifully. There were plenty of sirens wailing day and night but we in Barford hardly heard them. The Salisbury Cathedral had been built hundreds of years ago on five rivers. Its tall spire served as a marker for the enemy who were constantly bombing the ports of Portsmouth and Southampton to the south of us. The glow of fires could be seen at night from these ports. We had to consider ourselves fortunate.

Final exams were now imminent and so in the summer of 1942 I sat my school certificate. This was the equivalent of graduation I suppose, though there were never any such elaborate celebrations. Guess what? I failed! Surprise, surprise. So back I had to go in September to sit it again. This meant a whole term of classes with a small group in the hopes that we would get more concentrated teaching. Well, we didn't. For me it was an utter waste of time. I re-sat the exam at Christmas and failed again. Goodbye Godolphin!

Leaving Home

In January of 1943 I was sent to a Domestic Science school in the southwest of England to learn how to cook, clean, wash and generally run a house. Leaving home was quite the most ghastly experience. I wept at least two days beforehand and all the way in the train to Axminster where we were met and driven to a lovely old house in the country. Desperately homesick, I somehow managed to survive.

Mrs. Francillon, the head of the school, was an elderly woman but greatly in command of all her "*gells*". She had adopted a one-year-old girl and one of the sewing mistresses seemed to be in charge of that department. We were taught cooking by two women who were I suppose lesbians (I didn't even know of that word or life in those days). They were both pretty fierce.

The "*larndry*", as Mrs. Francillon called it, was a bit more relaxed. We had to wash various items. Ironing tablecloths with a flat iron heated on the stove was quite an endeavour. Spring-cleaning bathrooms and bedrooms was very structured, but I think I learnt quite a bit from this.

There were always two of us who spent a week being "drudges". This relieved us of classes but meant that we had to set the tables for meals, help serve and clear away, answer the doorbell and be gracious hostesses. I enjoyed this. Sewing was out of my league and I always complained that I didn't understand. The sewing mistress, in desperation, would complete the task for me.

Mrs. Francillon was very strict and did not allow makeup of any kind. On Saturday afternoons we could walk over the fields to Lyme Regis, usually armed with a dry jam sandwich. This took a good hour and we had to be back before dark. Exciting! However, I used to visit Mrs. Clarke, who had been so good to Martin when he had been stationed in Lyme. She was a dear dumpy little woman and I felt so secure under her wing. The war seemed miles away.

Mother wrote every week and once even Father wrote in his tiny, tidy handwriting.

We took an exam at the end of the year, both written and practical. The aim was to get a first class, which was 80 percent or more. If you didn't you were considered a failure! Guess what? I got 79 percent. Good old 2nd class Doreen.

Mrs. Francillon wrote a very nice letter to Mother saying what a nice girl I was.

Big Deal.

Employment

I was pleased to be home again, but what next? All I really wanted to do was to push prams in Hyde Park in London with other people's beautiful babies in them. There was a training school for this career known as the Norland Nannies. Unfortunately they were not in operation due to the war. Mother had seen an advertisement for help at a wartime day nursery in Salisbury that had been set up for mothers who would then be able to work in munitions factories. I applied and was accepted. Little did I realize that this actually was set up as a training school for nursery nurses. It was a two-year course, both practical and academic. Mother found me a room not far from the nursery where Miss Clark took me in as a paying guest. She was a funny old stick, but very kind and she fed me well.

I loved it at the nursery. At first there was just one prefab building that housed the babies, toddlers, kitchen, dining room and matron's office. It all soon had to be enlarged and another prefab building was added, so now there was the baby nursery, toddlers and, in the new building, the "tweenies". I loved it all and was totally happy.

During this time I also volunteered to teach first aid to young cadets through St John Ambulance. That terrified me, yet I quite enjoyed it. Anne also wrote from North Africa saying I was doing nothing for the war effort and that I should go and give blood. This of course I did and promptly passed out on the tiled hospital floor.

The war was progressing across North Africa and things were definitely looking more hopeful. At home we always left the garden door open at night, just in case one of my siblings had been given leave and might arrive and not wish to wake Mother and Father.

What a hope!

ANDRÉ

First Love

I always went home on weekends. The nursery closed at 1pm on Saturdays and I would either cycle the six miles home or catch a bus. One such weekend I returned home to find a visitor—Andre Figuiere from North Africa. Well, as night follows day, we fell in love!

He was nineteen and I was eighteen. Perhaps it was the war, or the knowledge that he had some connection with Anne and Martin, or just the fact that our hormones were in full swing. Don't ask, but we were so in love. He came as often as he could get away from his Free French parachute training. My parents became so fond of him and Mother spoke French with him, which made him feel even more part of the family. He in turn loved my parents and it really was such a happy interlude in my life. We went for walks together over the downs, loving the countryside and somehow getting to know one another even through a bit of a language barrier. He was much better at speaking English than I at French. He was Catholic, which bothered me a little as I knew my parents would be hesitant about me forming a lasting relationship. However, ties became too strong and we secretly became engaged. No real thought on my part as to our future. The war was still on, he was in the army and we were all alive and that was seemingly all that mattered.

Then one day we both came to our senses. I could not think of raising children in the Catholic belief; Andre realized that he must return to North Africa, where life would be too different for me. It was one of the most devastating moments in our lives. How were we going to survive without each other? It had to be. Eventually the day came when he was to return to North Africa. Andre came to the nursery to say goodbye. I can see it all now as we stood at the gate with tears streaming down our faces, promising to keep in touch. How gut-wrenching losing your first love is!

During the next three years, Andre wrote from North Africa telling me of his life in medical school, sending me sprigs of mimosa and eventually sending photos of his fiancée. Well I knew it was inevitable and in a way I was pleased for him. I knew we were not meant to be together.

Homecoming

At about the same time we heard that the hospital Anne was with had followed the liberating Allied forces into Greece, only to be surrounded by rebel forces in Athens. Anne was virtually a prisoner of war. I was devastated and wept in the nursery kitchen. The cook tried to comfort me but I was so scared. Mother, of course, was a tower of strength. She must have felt worse than me, but she was always so positive and had such faith. It was not a long-lasting affair. We were so relieved when the Allies liberated them again.

In 1944, at the beginning of June, I was woken by the sound of endless heavy traffic lumbering along the main road in Salisbury towards the coast. Could this be the anticipated launching of our forces to liberate Europe? How thankful I was that Martin, Bryan and Anne were still in the Mediterranean theatre of war where the Allies were advancing through Italy with reasonable confidence. This new venture I felt was going to be crucial. It was and many, many lives were lost in this brave attempt on June 6. However it proved the turning point of the war and by 1945 peace was declared. I rode my bike home from Salisbury to Barford on that very day, marvelling at the fact that my brothers and sister would return and that we could turn on lights again without fear.

The feeling was overpowering. Celebrations went on all over England. Whole streets and villages got together, pooling food and dancing the nights away with lights shining out of every window. Eventually Martin, Bryan and Anne all came home. It was unbelievable.

Mother organized a dinner party for us all. She felt it might be a little much for Maude so she asked one of the village girls to come and help. Dear Muriel had a cleft palate and I knew Mother was very sympathetic towards her. Muriel helped serve the main course and then came a choice of desert. When Muriel got to

Martin she politely said, "*Mi-er Mar-in, whish will you have, cho-let jung-et or orr-ange jellee*"?

Martin's face was blank; he had no idea what she was talking about. As usual I was stifling laughter at the vague look on Martin's face, which was such a typical expression he would put on to make us laugh. Mother, as always, came to the rescue and very firmly said, "Martin, which would you like, chocolate junket or orange jelly?" Mother was never allowed to forget this and her choice of deserts for poor Muriel to pronounce.

After supper we played demon patience, all six of us round the dining room table. It was never a racing kind. We all helped each other to get it out, and that night we did. It was memorable.

So here we all were again but of course none of us were the same. Anne, Martin and Bryan had travelled the world almost, lived through horrors and unnatural circumstances and come home to what must have seemed a very tame sort of life even if it felt secure. Mother and Father had lived through the terror of potentially losing one of their children, not knowing where they were at times, yet constantly writing to them from the security of their home, probably subconsciously trying to assure them of their inevitable return to safety. I had grown from a very sheltered teenager to a slightly more mature adult. Yes, we had changed because of the different lives we had all lived through these war years. Maude perhaps seemed the only one who had not changed. That ever-strong secure person in our lives who was forever there for us no matter what happened. How lucky we all were to have that great stability. We were once more our family unit, yet now we were all strangers, to a degree, amongst each other.

With the war over, rationing was still in effect. Things only gradually began to feel slightly more normal. Anne went to work in London as a secretary to Lady Louis Mountbatten at St. John's house. She and Hazel rented a flat in Earl's Court. Martin went to an agricultural college, which my uncle Colin had advised. There was not much call for art at this time unless Martin was prepared to do commercial which he was not. Bryan went to Oxford to study for the church.

Meanwhile I was finishing my course at the nursery and Matron advised me to go on and do my general nursing training. I was horrified. Not a hospital! Not in that place where I had fainted! No, I knew I couldn't face any of it. Matron persisted and suggested that I go to her training school at Hastings in Sussex for three months—if I didn't like it then I could give it up. She knew the matron there and knew it to be an excellent training hospital on par with the "London Hospital". Well, perhaps I could cope with just three months, so I reluctantly applied.

HOMECOMING.
BACK ROW - MARTIN. BRYAN. MAUDE. DOREEN. BILL
FRONT ROW - CATHERINE MOTHER FATHER ANNE

A Nurse in the Making

I was asked to go for an interview with the matron at Royal East Sussex Hospital, known as the RESH. I was terrified. Why on earth couldn't I just stay and be a nanny somewhere? I found the hospital, a huge sprawling red brick building up on a hill overlooking the town and the sea. Oh the smell of the interior was so awful, reminding me of Salisbury hospital where I had given blood. There was no way I could cope with this. Matron was huge, towering over me with a frilly cap on her head that finished in a ruffle round her neck. She was quiet and very composed with a kind smile. After talking to me for a while, she must have seen how terrified I was with absolutely *no* self-confidence. She walked with me to the top of stone steps leading down to the road and just said, "Right Miss Blyth, we'll see you on January 26."

"Unless anything unforeseen happens," I replied, hardly able to look at her and hoping to goodness that that would be my saviour.

It was not to be. So on January 26, 1946, I arrived at the nurses' home of the RESH to be shown my room by Home Sister. My name was on the door but I told her my initial was not "N" but "D". Home Sister explained that the N stood for nurse. My heart sank. Home Sister was small, severe looking and in charge. She also over-pronounced her S's, an affliction I immediately found fascinating.

Soon others arrived. This was the start of a new batch of nurses to begin their Preliminary Training School. We were issued our uniform and shown how to make up our caps. This to me was my first stumbling block. In all my three years of training, I never could master that art.

Every morning after breakfast we were assigned to a ward where we reported in to the sister at 9am. Our duties then consisted of giving out bedpans and wash water, washing backs of patients, helping a nurse make beds, turning patients, learning how to put in clean sheets, and rubbing pressure areas. When all this was done we had to pull out the beds from the wall while the maids dusted and swept, then push the beds back again, making sure that all bed wheels were turned inwards.

Then it would be time to give out "the drinks", which was tea, hot chocolate or milk. We did this from a trolley with a nurse so that we could learn to be observant of which patient could have what. Perhaps some needed to be fed or helped. This was our task. We stayed on the ward for just one and half hours, but in that time we learnt so much about not only the hospital routine but also about the patients, the people and how they felt, how they reacted to you, and how, by some simple smile or action, you could relieve them of anxiety or somehow make them feel better.

I had been assigned to a women's ward. Though I was still frightened of everything and everyone, I started to feel that there was a part of me that could help someone and this became so satisfying. The rest of the day during those first three months was taken up in the class room where we learnt anatomy and physiology and how to do simple procedures like attending to pressure areas and making a patient generally comfortable. With a life-sized doll (Annie was her name!) and a bed in the classroom, we were taught the right way to turn a patient and to make a bed *with* the inevitable hospital corners. Sister Worth, our sister tutor, was a great teacher. About twelve of us started the course.

By the end of the three months seven of us remained after we had sat our preliminary exams. I passed!

Then came the realization that we were on our way to being taught the rules and regulations of nursing. We worked from 7.30am to 8.30pm with three hours off in the day and half hours for lunch and supper. In the mornings we had 15 minutes for coffee and in that time we had to walk to the nurses' home and make our beds. The routine was rigid. Fear ruled my life. At this stage we were all juniors and given the lowliest tasks on the ward and were told in no uncertain terms if we were doing things the wrong way. We learnt that the ward sister was to be revered at all times and we never went off duty without presenting ourselves to her to ask permission. I suppose the routine saved my life. I could cope with that, but if things happened out of that routine I was terrified.

I made three great friends—Vicky, Barnes and Walker. Without these three I would never have survived. We supported each other and were able to see the funny side of things. Most nights we would make tea and gather in my room to discuss the day and laugh. All this lightened the load tremendously.

After four months on day duty we were assigned to a different ward for night duty. Another hurdle to get over. As juniors we ran between two wards, helping our senior nurse in either ward wherever she needed us. This was from 8pm until 8.30am, and we had supper in the ward kitchen. When ready to go off duty, we had to change into a clean apron, march down the long ward and ask sister if we may go off duty. Dropping with fatigue!

At this point our rooms were moved to the top floor to be quiet and we would collapse into hot baths with taps running and fall asleep until we heard Home Sister calling out and banging on doors, "*Nurssse, who'sss in thisss bathroom, turn off your tapsss, watersss cassscadin' over the gratin'.*" Yes, below the overflow a pipe was a grating that led into the door of the home.

We progressed, gradually taking on more responsibility, which for me was terrifying. I was scared of doing wrong and of my seniors. Terrified that I would not or could not do what was asked of me. Scared of being unable to meet a crisis and scared of letting a sick person down. Yet the satisfaction I received at times was overwhelming and it was the one thing that kept me going.

The first time I became a senior on night duty, I was alone apart from a junior "runner". Walking up the stone steps to the top where the night sister awaited me to tell me which ward was mine was one of the most agonizing moments. What was ahead of me? Could I cope? All night long doing my best, answering to the night sister when she did her rounds, writing reports and then, when I was at my lowest ebb, answering to the day sister as she questioned all I had done.

There were many lighter moments of course. The day I was asked to shave a male patient who was going to the operating room for surgery to a perforated gastric ulcer. Poor man was in agony. When I turned back the sheet to start shaving, I noticed his penis was up the other way! I was dumbfounded, but went about my duty as I had been told. It was not easy. Afterwards, I felt it my duty to tell the staff nurse my observations. I was concerned. When I told her that I thought this man had a deformity—well, I was never allowed to forget it. Even the sister laughed at me. I was so naive; I'd never had sex. Andre, my former fiancé, had only said one day that he wanted to give me a baby. I had no real idea where he would get it from, but anyway I didn't want it at the time. Mother had given me books on chickens and eggs but I never really caught on to *that*—and, come to think of it never, have.

Probably because the four of us had such riotous times after work in my bedroom, when I returned from holiday at some point my room had been moved to the sisters' quarters right next door to Home Sister's room. This put paid to our tea parties in my room but, no matter, we just went on somewhere else. However when Home Sister used her sink, it used to gurgle in mine. One day she stopped me and said, "*Nurssse Blyth, doesss my water make asss much noissse asss your water when it runsss away?*" Poor Home Sister! She often took prayers in the chapel after day duty, which, if we attended the second supper, we were obliged to attend. We were always exhausted so very prone to hysterics. If the four of us happened to be there together it was fatal. As Dora progressed through the lordsss prayer, spitting her way through all the sss's, we would be helpless and Walker's low-moaning giggle was beyond the pale. Stifling everything, tears would be rolling down our faces. We then had to march out of the chapel and were bid goodnight by both Home Sister and Matron, who stood rigidly at the end of the corridor.

On Tuesdays after lunch we had to line up outside the kitchen and the assistant matron doled out to each one their four ounces of margarine and two ounces of butter for the week. Father had given me an old communion wafer tin in which I carried my ration about. In November we had to line up in the same way to stir the Christmas pudding and make a wish. Many wishes must have been the same. No one was allowed to have holidays or days off at Christmas, which was a really fair way to do it. So we were *all* on duty over the holiday. Christmas morning started with the day staff gathering in the front hall, our capes turned inside out so that the red showed. Matron led the procession, which went through the entire hospital singing carols. It really was pretty impressive. In the afternoon some of us nurses would perform half hour skits in each ward in front of patients and visitors. These skits had been well rehearsed and vetted by Matron. All the wards chose a different theme as far as decorations went. Depending on the imagination and capability of that ward's nursing staff they were often fantastic.

The eye wards and the theatre had been damaged by bombs during the war, and the hospital was anxious to get them up and running again. When it came to my turn to work there, the theatre had just been opened, but there were no spotlights. So during an eye operation with a sister assisting, I had to stand and point a flashlight right onto the eye while the surgeon operated on it. I became green many times and had to breathe deeply to stop myself from passing out. Eyes never will be my forte.

In the end I enjoyed the men's ward best of all. Theatre had no appeal for me; in fact when I finally refused to scrub for an appendix I was sent to Matron. I was amazed at myself for being able to tell her that I had no intention of continuing my nursing career in the operating theatres and that she could move me out at any time. I had never come across such a bunch of arrogant, selfish men as some of those surgeons were and I suddenly was not about to be put down by them. It was all so impersonal. I hated it.

"Casualty" or "emerg" was fun and it was run by a dragon of a sister who was deaf and a cockney. She also ran the outpatient department. One day I was assigned to run the circumcision clinic and Sister Chase presented me with a bottle with colourless liquid in it. She told me, "*sayve all ve foreskins, nurse.*"

Well we did as we were told, so every bit of foreskin after each procedure was dumped into this bottle. At the end of this horrendous clinic I presented Sister Chase with the bottle, which she put in her fridge along with her butter ration and emerg pint of blood! A few days later a man came in with a very badly lacerated finger. Sister Chase examined it as I took the rough dressing off. She immediately got out the little bottle. After I had cleaned this laceration to her satisfaction, she plunked a piece of foreskin on it and I then had to bandage all in place.

As the man walked out Sister Chase said, quite within his hearing, "*Well oi ope e don't get ve sayme sensaytion.*"

The finger healed miraculously. It was my introduction to plastic surgery.

ROYAL EAST SUSSEX HOSPITAL GRADUATION.

We sat our final hospital exams. Vicky and I were awarded top practical nursing honours. That was quite a thrill. But still the state exams were ahead of us. After sitting these, we fearfully waited for results. The mail came and our envelopes were laid out on the table. A fat envelope was a sign that you could apply to re-sit. My envelope was thin! I was now a State Registered Nurse and allowed to possess the drug cupboard keys. I was in shock and over the moon—maybe I had finally overcome my lack of self-confidence. I could hardly wait to phone home and say to Mother and Father, "This is Nurse Blyth, State registered nurse speaking." Tears ran down my face.

I acquired another boyfriend, Hugh, whom I had nursed as a hemophiliac. We did actually become engaged and he gave me a ring, but I knew deep down that I would spend my life looking after his hemorrhages and wondered if I was really prepared for that. I knew also that my family saw this and was scared for me.

Throughout my time at RESH in Hastings, I was so lucky to be able to visit a dear friend of my parents. Denny had worked for my grandparents as a nurse to my mother's younger siblings when they lived in Egypt, where my grandfather was the head of customs in Alexandria. Mother was born and raised in Egypt, where she met Father who was a priest at Mena House. When Mother turned 19, she became engaged to Father.

Nurse Denny had since become the district nurse in Hythe, Kent. During my childhood, we often went to Hythe for holidays. It was about a two-hour bus ride from Hastings to Hythe, so when I had three nights off in a row I would board the bus for Hythe. Here was a haven of peace and comfort. Denny always wanted to hear all about my training and we chatted in front of the fire over tea. She fed me great meals and always brought my breakfast in bed to me. She really spoilt me. I loved her dearly.

My parents and family were tremendously supportive throughout my training. Without them I know I could never have got through it. Martin, Bryan and Anne all were married during those three years. I was able to get short times off to attend the three weddings, though after the third Matron asked me if this was to be all! Anne married Rodney whom she had met on board the ship going out to North Africa. Martin married Betty, who was the daughter of a parson my parents had known when Father was in Milton. Bryan married Catherine, whom he had met during the war.

Father retired and they had to move from our beloved Barford. They bought a house, tiny in comparison to the rectory, in

Weymouth where both my brothers had been born. I have no idea how they got rid of all the stuff, or how they moved. Maude of course was as usual her tower of strength and moved in to the little house with them. But we all began to see the writing on the wall. Maude was no longer needed by my parents, who could not afford to keep her. She went to another position with her friend and I visited her there. It was heartbreaking for everyone. As well, our home seemed to have lost something secure and precious, never to be the same.

As far as the Royal East Sussex Hospital went, I longed to stay there where at last I had become to feel secure. I had been successful and was being encouraged by the sisters to take up a position as a staff nurse. The sisters were all RESH-trained. I could see myself falling into that same pattern. No, there was more to life than that.

I didn't know how to deliver a baby, so how could I call myself a nurse? The RESH was not a well-known London hospital. I felt that in order to progress I must get a name behind myself, so I applied to Queen Charlotte's Hospital, the biggest teaching maternity hospital in England. Matron was hesitant when I told her, but hoped I would be happy.

Call the Midwife

Between leaving the RESH and starting my maternity training, Walker and I decided to branch out. She came to live with us in Weymouth and we tried to get a nine-to-five job working in casualty at the local hospital. As State Registered Nurses, we felt they would give us anything we asked for. Wrong!

So we decided to quit nursing and work in a beachfront hotel. We changed our names. Why? I have no idea. Walker was Sally— the waitress. I was Jill—the chambermaid. Of course it was more shift work and deadly. However we both saw the funny side of things. The headwaiter kept yelling her name to which she never answered because she wasn't really Sally. We both ate our meals in the staff dining room and this proved to be hilarious. The shoe cleaning man used to eat porridge for breakfast and every time he opened his mouth his teeth dropped down and the spoon went between his teeth and his gums.

One day we lined up for lunch and were given a plateful of beef, spuds and veggies, but no gravy. I spied the gravy on the back of the stove, so poured it liberally and proudly over my food. As I started to eat, gloating over my find, I realized that it was black coffee! Chambermaiding, I learnt a lot about how people can behave whilst on holiday: the mess they left to clean up was sometimes unforgivable. I walked around with a string of master keys around my waist and made sure I knew when anyone was leaving so that I could grab the tip.

Walker and I didn't last too long in that career and went on a tandem bicycling tour of northern France. That was an experience and loads of fun. We cycled down the Champs-Elysees in shorts, which was not quite the thing to do for ladies. We also went on a holiday to Corsica. It was a package deal. Horizon Holidays flew us out and we camped on the beach in tents. Food was provided. We went for two weeks and loved every minute of it.

It was here that I met Basil. Being in the Mediterranean, the weather was gorgeous, the swimming perfect and we had wine with every meal. Basil was the best dancer. We danced on the tiny concrete pad on the beach every night. We kept our stupid phony names so forever afterwards I was Jill to Basil!

In February 1949, Martin and Betty's Wendy was born in Weymouth.

Time to start again and I began at Queen Charlotte's Hospital in London in September of 1949. The hospital had been bombed so not all of the building was functional. There were several floors each with six six-bedded wards presided over by a sister and staff nurse. The top (seventh) floor was for labour and delivery. We did two months of day duty in a six-bedded ward, the first month as a junior and the second as a senior. There were two to each ward.

This was followed by two months of night duty and two months of day and nights on the top floor. Mothers had to stay in bed after delivery for 10 days, so we were always running around with water and bedpans. We also had to bathe the babies and sew a new binder over the umbilical cord area every day. When a woman was about to be delivered, the staff nurse would open the ward door and yell, "BABY," whereupon we had to drop everything and fly up to the top floor to witness the delivery. We had to witness twenty deliveries before we could participate ourselves. If your ward had a bed, it was up to you to transfer mother and babe to your care. It was like a cattle market, with up to 30 student nurses crammed into a small room watching a poor woman being delivered. I used to cringe at the inhumanity of it all.

In my second day term I was moved out of my ward and put as a junior in another ward. This amazed me. I had never been demoted in my nursing life. When I enquired of the unapproachable sister the cause of this demotion, she answered with her back to me, "Well nurse, you go about with such a worried look on your face that you harass the mothers and diminish their milk supply."

I was dumbfounded. I explained that I was worried because I couldn't do my work according to my standards. What should I do?

"Change your expression, nurse."

Would I ever become a midwife? To add to this, all the women in the other ward complained of hemorrhoids. I at once attributed this to my face.

I began to see why Matron at RESH had not been so encouraging for me to go to Queen Charlotte's. The standard of care was not what I was used to at all. It didn't scare me—it frustrated me. The labour and delivery floor was awful, probably more so because Queen Charlotte's received the most difficult maternity cases. The hydrocephalics—babies who had grown to full term with enlarged heads full of water—were the worst to me; the head was pierced to drain the fluid so that the baby could be delivered "normally" rather than via an "abnormal" C-section. This method seemed barbaric to me.

I was called for my first delivery at 3am, as it was "my turn". An intern was present which I at once felt unnecessary. However, he asked me if I knew what this was. I replied that it was my first delivery. He then persisted to question me and in the end he said the baby would have no back to its head and that eventually it would die, but that at first it would cry, so I must put a pad of cotton wool over its face so that the mother would believe it had been a stillborn. I was horrified and refused, saying that he could do that. He said he was a Catholic and it was against his religion to take a life. As the baby emerged, he handed me the pad. As I bathed the mother afterwards, we both wept.

Anne and Rodney were living at this time at Elm Park Gardens in London and they had just had Peter. I don't think I would have survived Queen Charlotte's Hospital without them. Their flat was an oasis for me and I loved spending my days off there, helping Anne with Peter.

This first part of the midwifery course lasted six months but we were not yet qualified to do home deliveries. Having, amazingly enough, passed the course, I looked around for somewhere else to do the second part. This I found in Woking where a doctor was starting to teach natural childbirth. What a change greeted me.

This was a small hospital and a happy place. After a week's orientation I was sent to Woolwich for three months to learn the "district work". I lived in a home with other district nurses and had a midwife over me to teach me. I had a bike, black bag and gas and air machine. We did prenatal clinics and visited the homes to make sure they had all that was needed. It was such a great experience. I loved it and learnt so much. Delivering a lovely cockney lady in her front room with the Aspidistra, I eyed the fireplace where I hoped to burn the afterbirth. The fireplace looked as if it had never been used. My heart sank—what to do with the thing. She read my mind and said, "*Don't put it ahtside nurse cos ve cats'll ave it!*" So I had to wrap the afterbirth in newspaper and tuck it under my arm, carrying the rest of the paraphernalia and swing on a tram that was carrying all the workers to work at the Woolwich arsenal. The only fear I had was that it might start to drip.

During the last three months of this course we worked in the hospital. There were two Barts nurses in our class with whom we really didn't associate much. Barts, or St. Bartholomew's, nurses had been trained at the selective namesake hospital in London and seemed far above us somehow.

However, one day one of them, Jean Robertson, known as Robbie, asked if I would like to go to Canada with her. Well I was a bit dumbfounded. First of all I was not sure where exactly Canada was. I remembered that they grew wheat somewhere but that was about all. Secondly, why was she asking me? Anne was expecting her second baby and I had promised her that I would help her when the baby came in February of 1951. I was due to finish my course at the end of February but I had promised to stay with Anne for three months. Could Robbie wait that long? Robbie was agreeable. So we tentatively planned to go in June 1951.

First, Bryan and Catherine's Janet was born that January.

Then, Anne and Rodney's Caroline was duly born. I was so pleased to be with them all. We had a wonderful three months. I enjoyed every minute. Caroline was a very demanding baby and so different from the placid Peter. We could see right from the start that no grass would grow under her feet.

My parents, who had to give up the house in Weymouth, had gone to live for a short while with Martin and Betty in Devizes. Then Father was offered some casual work at St Mark's parish in Salisbury plus a house to live in. They moved here but were not entirely happy. I thought it time in their lives that they could feel settled. June was fast approaching and I was having second thoughts about Canada. No, I *must* see my parents settled. So Robbie and I postponed everything till September. In July we found a house and I helped my parents buy it and move in. I worked then in a fearful nursing home in Salisbury and lived at home.

Now September was looming and I was, yet again, unable to commit myself to Robbie and Canada. Unwilling to wait any longer for me, Robbie left and I promised her I would follow in April of 1952. That September Father became acutely ill and, after medical and surgical treatment, he died of heart failure on October 16th. This was one of the things I had never wanted to be part of—my father's death. Emotionally it was beyond me even to think about it. Yet I was the only one with my mother at the time. She taught me so much strength at that time.

Why had I procrastinated over my trip to Canada? I shall never know.

Canada Calls

With all these sad details behind me, I decided to stay at home with Mother and do a Plastic Surgery course at Odstock hospital near Salisbury. I learnt to drive Father's car, so I was pretty independent and could also drive Mother about. I started making plans for my eventual voyage to Canada, passports and transportation etc. Somehow I found a freighter that was to leave Glasgow for Montreal at the end of March 1952. I booked a passage on it. Walker promised to drive me there and I bade Hugh goodbye saying that I would return in a year. Mother all the while was so encouraging and I never thought for one moment how unselfish she was being.

There are some people who change the course of your life completely. The first in my life was my mother who found the day nursery for me and was always a source of tremendous strength to me. The second was the matron at that nursery who pushed me into general nursing. The third was the matron of RESH, Royal East Sussex Hospital, who was so knowledgeable and caring.

The fourth was Robbie. She expected me to keep my promise of joining her and she was on the dock in Montreal as we sailed in that April of 1952.

The freighter was of the Donaldson line. The officers and crew were Scottish, a great bunch of people. After leaving the Clyde and getting over seasickness, I thoroughly enjoyed the trip. I shared a cabin with a Scottish lass who was joining her husband in Toronto. She wept as we sailed down the Clyde. I was not in the least bit homesick which was so unusual for me. I became friendly with two of the officers, one being Bob Durling and the other I don't remember. I had never been at sea before. The whole experience thrilled me. Before we disembarked, the immigration chap came aboard, stamped my passport with "landed immigrant" and that was that!

I had travelled with a steamer trunk, not giving a thought as to how I would transport it once on land. However, Robbie had it all in hand and away we went in a taxi to the Rockhill Apartments on Cote de Neige road in Montreal, where Robbie had been living with Vida, a Canadian nurse from Calgary for the past six months. Robbie immediately took me to a supermarket. I just gasped. There was a whole display of red meat ready for sale! Could we buy this? I had never seen anything like it. England was still rationed. I realized then I was in a different world and I liked what I saw!

The apartment was decorated entirely in orange and it belonged to some Hungarian count, who had gone off to Hungary for a year and rented it out to us for very little. Robbie's cousins lived downstairs, so it was really to them that we owed this bit of luck. Robbie and Vida had been working at the Royal Victoria Hospital in Montreal, and attached to this prestigious hospital was the Montreal Neurological Institute. Here Robbie had transferred herself and somehow got me a position there too. Once again I was a bit scared, as I had never done any of this kind of nursing before. Our apartment was not too far from the hospital and we *could* walk to it over Mount Royal, however it *was* quicker to catch a bus.

Montreal

The Montreal Neurological Institute, or MNI, was a place I shall never forget. It had a unique atmosphere of calm and hope. I put this down to the two people who were really at the head of the whole institution: Doctor Wilder Penfield and the matron, Miss Flanagan. Under these two were the heads of departments, surgeons, doctors and nurses. Among them were qualified doctors who were doing post-graduate work in neurosurgery or neurology. They were from all parts of the world and were a wonderful bunch of people. I was assigned to a neurosurgery ward, first with women and later with men. Most of the patients were suffering from head injuries or epilepsy, and all were subject to horrendous seizures. It was a nurse's job to witness and write detailed accounts of these seizures. These included notes on whether a patient's eyes moved to the left or right, whether their limbs twitched and, if so, whether to the right or left, if and when became unconscious, and exactly how long their symptoms lasted. With these notes Dr. Penfield was able to ascertain what part of a patient's brain was being affected, and could then decide if surgery to remove the scarred area would be possible. He did rounds with his interns and was always so caring and quiet and ready to acknowledge us for work we had well-tabulated or witnessed. I loved it all. It was so rewarding.

I managed to spend one of my days off in the operating room watching Dr. Penfield. The operation lasted for eight hours and I had no idea how the time had flown. Under local anaesthetic, he went in to the patient's brain, located the scar tissue and then proceeded to tell the patient exactly what he was going to do, warning the patient he might experience difficulty in speaking for a few days. (The patient's scar tissue was on the brain's speech centre.) Then Dr. Penfield proceeded to remove the scarring. I nursed that patient afterwards and watched his slow but successful recovery.

Our social life was great. We hosted many parties at the Rockhill and they included doctors and ditch diggers and all got along just fine. It was a complete eye opener for me. Life was relaxed and fun, there was plenty to eat and drink, and no one got upset. We three shared a bed and a camp-cot but, as we all were on different shifts, it never seemed a problem. Vida fascinated me. Before she went on duty she always curled her eyelashes with a grotesque piece of equipment. I ate like a pig and was nearly at the point when I was going to have to up my board payment, when Vida one morning produced pancakes, bacon and maple syrup. That did it. It must have formed some sort of cement in my stomach as my appetite slowly subsided.

We spent a day in the Laurentians but the snow had almost melted so no skiing. Montreal was fine but somehow I began to feel restless. I had suddenly realised that there was a vast continent stretching out to a sea on the far side of the country. We began to talk and eventually Robbie saw an ad from the GM factory in Oshawa, Ontario asking for drivers to take their new Chevrolets to Vancouver. It was apparently cheaper than freighting them. Vida had worked at Shaughnessy Hospital in Vancouver and told us it was the place to work. We applied to GM.

We didn't really think too much about future plans, we just went with the flow, work, parties, apartment cleaning, washing etc. Then one day it came! We had been accepted by GM to drive a brandnew Chevrolet from Oshawa to Vancouver. Vida had a driver's license but Robbie and I had only just got ours in England and of course we had never driven on the right hand side of the road in our lives. So off to the Motor Vehicle office in Montreal. Here we were given forms to fill out, "colour of eyes, colour of hair, height weight, name and DOB." (One of the doctors at MNI had filled out one pertaining to his dog and actually got a license for his dog to drive!) We pushed the completed paper through a wicket and a book with a scotch-taped crucifix on it was pushed back to us with a request to "swear that you know how to drive a car."

Of course we did as bid.

"Two dollars and fifty cents."

You bet! We were now legit Canadian drivers.

On Vida's advice, Robbie and I applied to Shaughnessy Hospital in Vancouver and were both accepted. It all seemed so simple.

My family at home, especially Mother who wrote to me every week, were so supportive. I had received word from Andre that he was married and had a son. I pretty well wrote him off! Hugh was ever anxious for my safety and Mother wrote telling me to take care as she was sure that there were "Red Indians"—an old-fashioned term, now considered highly offensive, for Native Americans—still about in Canada. Basil still kept in touch with his "Jill."

On the Road

Before Vida, Robbie and I set off on this new adventure, we had to give our notices (sadly in a way), have a farewell party and visit New York. We had the party and I can still recall the deadly feeling the next morning as we boarded a Greyhound bus bound for New York. It seemed to take forever, but I think we slept most of the way. We stayed in the YWCA and did NYC in a flash, including Radio City Music Hall, Times Square and the show *The King and I*.

What a whirlwind it was.

Then back on the bus to Montreal; pack up and away on another bus to Oshawa. I guess my trunk came with us, goodness knows how. We stayed at the YWCA in Oshawa where we met a lady who worked at the radio station in Hamilton. Evidently this was on our route west and she seemed intrigued with our plans and asked us to drop in at the station. Having never been in one before, we thought it might be fun.

Next morning we got to the GM factory and a gleaming 1952 Chevy was brought out to us. Vida and I were in identical outfits and Robbie had her Barts' basket and brown betty teapot. Some Ontario newspaper took our photos.

Robbie climbed in the Chevy and asked where it started. I felt sure that this lack of knowledge would sink us, so I enquired as to whether we should take off the distributor cap if we were to park the car anywhere. Father had taught me this in the war so that if Nazis parachuted down, they couldn't take the car. I had no idea where or what the distributor cap was but I thought it sounded knowledgeable.

The answer I got was, "Oh gee Miss, if they want it that bad, let 'em have it—there's plenty more in the factory!"

With that, loaded down, we set off down the Queen Elizabeth Way highway to Toronto, Robbie at the wheel and all of us in hysterics. A road sign said that we must do at least 30 miles an hour so as not to impede traffic. We were doing about 20 at the most. It was all pretty terrifying.

First stop was the Hamilton Radio Station. Here the three of us were ushered into a room and introduced to a lady named Jane Grey who was sitting at a desk with a red light in front of her. She asked us a lot of questions as to who we were and where we had been working and exclaimed, "Oh, under that wonderful Doctor Wilder Penfield!"—which we thought a trifle odd. After all this interrogation, she said, "Now listeners, these gals are going to cross the Rockies. If you have any advice for them, please phone in to the radio station and you can talk to them."

We were mortified to think we had been on the air and had broadcast our revered doctor's name. As we left her broadcasting room we were called to phones ringing here, there and everywhere. It was wild!

In the end I met Robbie in the corridor. She said, "Let's get out of here, this woman on the phone has told me not to go over the High Moon mountains 'cos that's where her son-in-law lost his spare parts and I don't even know where our spare parts are."

We hightailed it to the car, now fondly known as Bessy the beige Chevrolet, started it but couldn't move it. Technicians were catcalling out of the station windows and finally yelled, "Try the emergency!"

Vida interpreted for us—the handbrake.

We were highly disciplined. Each one of us drove only for 100 miles at a stretch, then moved to the back seat to relax, while the navigator drove. We passed in and out of the States, crossing borders with little difficulty. The Trans-Canada Highway was not yet fully opened. We started early in the morning and by 4pm we were looking for suitable cheap motels with an eatery nearby. It was a wonderful trip. Driving through the Badlands of South Dakota was impressive, as were the miles of prairie country where we began to meet real cowboy-looking people. We had one flat tyre, and did an oil change which was mandatory. Apart from that, Bessy carried us like a dream. We eventually got to Calgary where Vida's parents welcomed us. We stayed for a couple of nights.

Sadly we left Vida there and drove down through Washington state and up into the Okanagan where we stayed with Hazel, Anne's good friend who was a physio in Penticton. On then to Vancouver where, through Shaughnessy, we quickly found accommodation for ourselves, left our luggage and took Bessy to Duecks where she would go on the car lot. It had taken us two weeks to cross this vast continent and we had loved every minute of it, and now felt desperate at saying goodbye to our faithful steed. It is amazing, as I look back, how little we thought of insurance, sickness or accidents. How lucky we were.

Vancouver

Our newfound accommodation was a room at the top of an older house in the Shaughnessy area of Vancouver. This floor had two other bedrooms, which were also rented out, a bathroom and a kitchen in a sort of cupboard that we all shared. The bedroom had a dormer window, a cot and a pullout couch and crockery, all for 45 dollars a month!

The house was owned by an elderly lady and her housekeeper, and the rules were pretty strict such as no men after 10pm. They had a stuffed parrot in a cage halfway up the stairs which was "put to bed" every night with a cover over its cage. We were within walking distance of the hospital and, since we had arrived at the end of August, we had Labour Day weekend to get ourselves acquainted and sorted out.

Vancouver looked like a beautiful city, under towering mountains that went down to the sea and lovely beaches. We soon found our way around and hiked up Mount Hollyburn and picked blueberries, which we had never seen before. The view from this mountain was quite breathtaking. I felt very settled here.

Shaughnessy hospital was built primarily for war vets. It was huge with seven wards of seventy-six patients each, together with operating rooms and all the usual diagnostic areas. Miss Rossiter, Matron, welcomed us and assigned us to our wards. Robbie was on the top floor, South 3, and I was on the second floor, South 6. It had two wings with thirty-two beds in each, and two-bedded wards down the main corridor. The nurses' station was in the centre.

All the nurses were graduates. Shifts were eight hours. Orderlies did a lot of the heavy work, and most of the work pertaining to men. The head nurse, Mrs. North, was the most fantastic person and we all loved and respected her. Her deputy, Mary Rutledge, was desperately efficient and a slave driver but we all loved her too. It was one of the happiest places I have ever worked. Doctors were graduates, doing their year's internship before becoming full-fledged doctors. Everyone seemed young and a lot of fun.

We were so amazed at working eight-hour shifts (and not really working too hard at that either) that I wondered if we should apply to the hospital next door to do casual work, but then our free time became so valuable that we soon gave up that idea.

SHAUGHNESSY.

Life was really great. We joined the hospital choir and got ready for Christmas. We had boyfriends, who came and went. Two were brothers, Les and Humph, who took us to Seattle for a weekend— and their mother came too. What a hoot that was! Then there was Robbie's Steve, a physiotherapist, who didn't like peas and whenever he came to supper we always seemed to have them. We became quite stupidly hysterical over him. Then there were George and Andy. It was all rather superficial but a lot of fun.

Getting them down the stairs past the parrot without making any noise rather later than thought respectable was often hard.

Robbie and I went skiing several times. She was better at it than me. We both bought all the equipment and felt we looked like real pros. We were royally entertained by distant relations of Denny and had one of our two Christmas dinners that year with them; the other was with the delightful Scottish parents of Jimmy Morton who had befriended us in Montreal where he was doing his internship.

We also got in touch with a Chataway family living on Vancouver Island in Lantzville. They very kindly invited us over for the night. Harold was a doctor in Nanaimo, Pat was his wife, and they had a daughter, Nancy, and two sons, Dick and Martin. They were all younger than Robbie and I, a happy family who lived right on the water. We walked along the beach and they made us feel at home. I kept well in touch with all my family and friends back home, and Bob Durling wrote to say that the Donaldson Line was sailing round to Vancouver from Glasgow in February and that he hoped to see me again.

Home Again

That set us thinking. We had both said we would only be gone a year and Robbie was well over that year. Should we try and get on that freighter and go home? Neither of us really wanted to leave Shaughnessy or Vancouver. If I went home I was going to have to face Hugh who was waiting patiently for me. I kept looking at his ring, knowing that that was not for me and that I must finish the whole relationship and return the ring. I felt such a heel. So once more we gave our notices. As we bade farewell to Miss Rossiter, Robbie and I both dissolved into tears. Matron seemed nonplussed and then Robbie piped up and through her tears said, "We hate to leave, it's been one long party!"

Not exactly what Miss Rossiter had expected I think but she laughed. What a tremendous bunch of people they were: dedicated nurses and people, demanding the best from all yet so broadminded.

We gave up smoking and returned every bottle we could find to collect together the 400 dollars for the trip home. Somehow we packed all our gear, including my trunk, the skis, two whole hams wrapped in wax as meat was still rationed in England, and a crate of china (whole dinner service) for Mother as there was only white china to be had in England. A friend's husband worked at Canada Packers and secured us the hams. Our other great friends there included Elsie and Emil Juba. Just wonderful people. We boarded the freighter in Vancouver harbour, Andy and George brought us chocolates, and Les and Humph waved to us as we sailed under the Lions Gate Bridge heading for San Francisco!

There must have been quite a few passengers onboard as there was a doctor. All passengers seemed much older than us and they played a lot of shuffleboard. There was a pool on deck, small but great, and as we felt warmer going south we enjoyed a swim. It was sad leaving Vancouver. I wondered if I would ever see that suspension bridge we had crossed so many times to go skiing again, or those great mountains and the beautiful shoreline. This place had given me one of the happiest times of my life.

Our next excitement was the sight of the Golden Gate Bridge. We sailed under it and though it wasn't golden—a sort of reddish orange—it was still so impressive. We sailed up river to Stockton where Robbie and I went ashore and marveled at the shops. Our next port of call was San Pedro, which is close to Los Angeles. We were beginning to get quite pally with Bob Durling and the doctor, which added to the fun of the trip. Going through the Panama Canal in the daytime was amazing—a totally new experience. After the first set of locks we went through a very narrow part where there was a plaque secured into a rock along the shore, the point where the two excavating teams met, one from Panama and the other from Cristobal. This was dedicated to all those who had died in the building of the canal. Looking at the terrain, I marveled at their efforts. It was nothing but jungle and so many died of malaria.

On through Gatun Lake to the second set of locks and into the Caribbean Sea. Here we docked at the island of Curacao, which was so attractive with boats tied up along the shore, with their sails down over the produce that they had for sale. Brightly coloured vegetables and fruits and black, black people. Robbie, the doctor (wish I could remember his name), Bob and I went ashore and had a drink and watched all the local goings on. It was a lot of fun. During our sail through the Caribbean, I fell asleep on deck and both my shins were badly sunburnt. They developed huge blisters and the doctor decided to debride both legs. I think he just wanted something to do. Into the "hospital" I went, up on the table, and Robbie gave me a good shot of the best morphine in my arm. The purser came in to ensure fair play but I couldn't have cared less what they did to me. Once all the dirty stuff was over they wrapped my legs in plaster and carried me back to my bunk.

Here I had to remain for a few days to allow the swelling to go down and my legs to heal. My meals were brought to me, and Bob often came down to visit, usually after their supper. This of course was not allowed and one evening while he was in the cabin we heard all the officers and captain coming down to visit me too! There was no escape, so Bob stuffed himself into the clothes closet, getting more and more claustrophobic as their visit went by. Were they suspicious? Who knows? All was well in the end.

We eventually came to the Atlantic. I was up and about by then and begged them to take my plasters off. I was really getting panicky by the time we were nearing Liverpool. The day before we docked, the plasters came off. Farewells to all—which, after six weeks, was sad. Bob promised to keep in touch and asked me to write to his sister, Chris, who was a nurse in Glasgow and thinking of going to Canada. Robbie and I caught a train, bags and baggage, to Euston and there, walking away from me, were Mother and Anne. I tiptoed up behind them, put my arms around them and said, "Hi Mom, *yer look lahke* a million bucks!" They turned, Mother's face ashen—not my daughter with this dreadful accent. We all had a good laugh and a good hug.

It was great to be home amongst my family. First thing I had to do was contact Hugh. We met in Hyde Park and I returned his ring. I guess he had realized by my lack of correspondence that this was inevitable. I felt really badly for him. He needed someone to look after him but my visit to Canada made me realize that there was a life to be lived and it wasn't looking after poor old Hugh. Mother was still living in the little house they had moved into the year before when I had left. She seemed happy there and had many good friends and neighbours. She still did a lot of church work in Salisbury, so was very active. I felt happy about her.

Anne and family seemed happily settled in Stoke Poges. Martin and Betty had added Simon to their family and were living in Lewes where Martin was a car salesman for Dicksons garage. Art had become his sideline. Bryan was a full-fledged parson living in Bournemouth. He and Catherine had added Anita to their family. Maude had retired and was living in a dear little bungalow with Gladys who had been in service with Maude before I was born. They got along so well together and it was great to see Maude so happily settled without having to work so hard. They lived in Chipstead, Kent.

Back to Work

Next, find a job. I had thought I could work again with Robbie, but she went back to Barts, where only Barts-trained nurses were accepted on the staff. They had provided her with a flat in London so she was all set. I felt that London was where I had to be, so I applied to Lambeth Hospital as a staff nurse and was accepted.

What a dump! Security checks in and out, and almost across the street from the Elephant and Castle underground. I was allocated to a men's ward, which I actually loved, but there were no facilities like the ones I had gotten so used to in Shaughnessy. No occupational therapists, only a few physios. No rehab facilities.

A young man was brought in after a fall off some scaffolding paralyzed him from the waist down. It seemed that no one cared and that that was his fate. What about his bodily functions, his future, his family and, above all, his morale? I put my whole self into his care. I picked him up bodily and put him in a bath every day, made sure he had adequate pressure point care, dealt with bowel care, catheters, taught him how to hook a rug and, hopefully, gave support to his wife who had three small kids to cope with. This of course was together with the care of twenty other patients but none so critical as Fred. I began to think of rehab and knew he had to get to the rehab centre at Roehampton. I fought tooth and nail until finally he was transferred and, as if my stay in Lambeth had been fulfilled, I resigned and looked for another job.

During my stint in Lambeth, the one saving grace on my time off was that Basil had obtained a flat just around the corner from the hospital. I could walk there in the evenings and actually stayed there on weekends. Anne and Co. had moved to Stoke Poges, while Robbie was busy at Barts and with a new boyfriend. Basil, I realized long after, was gay. However, I felt so safe with him, he had such a great sense of humour, loved classical music and was also a great dancer. He and I had been to Corsica together before I went to Canada and we had had a great time together. He was such a good friend to me. I helped him redecorate the flat, wallpapering and painting—a big relief from the hospital. I was still and always "Jill" to him.

I scanned the nursing ads for a new job and decided it was time to move up the ladder, so answered an ad for a relief outpatient sister's post at Woolwich Memorial Hospital. I was accepted and felt terrified once again. The department was huge and quite modern. The sister I was relieving was in cahoots with the staff nurse so I was not too welcome. The staff nurse was Dutch and tough but gradually she came around and we got on well. She was really a very great help to me as she was used to the routine and the doctors and really ran a tight ship, which I had no argument with.

I enjoyed my time there except for the confines of the nurses' home. My room was fine, but the sitting room was only for sisters. They were a cliquey bunch and talked about nothing except the hospital. I got frustrated and bored with all this. It seemed the higher up you went in the nursing profession, the smaller your circle of friends became. Jo Mills, the OR sister, was the only bright spark among them. So eventually I enquired if I could live out. Unheard of! However, I persisted and found myself a room plus kitchen in a house in Blackheath, sharing a bathroom with three other people. What a relief to have my own place again, and I was already used to confined spaces.

My time as outpatient sister was coming to an end and I was then rotated to relieve sisters on other wards for brief periods such as holidays. This was excellent experience. I was also allowed to go on a sister's course at King Edward College in London for six weeks as long as I promised to return to Woolwich. It was all good experience though quite honestly I couldn't see myself spending the rest of my life as a sister. A sister is in charge of a ward and ranked above a staff nurse who, in turn, is ranked above a nurse. I was then asked to be the assistant night sister. The head one, Sister Conway, was fearful! How was I going to stand it all?

Well, I went for it. Wow, what an experience. It was a thirteen-hour-a-night job, with two nights off every two weeks. When the other night sister was off, I was on my own. Two hundred and fifty beds plus a casualty and a maternity wing were my responsibility, with only student nurses on duty—except in maternity. There were no nurses on duty in casualty. It was a frantic life. On top of all this, I had to do rounds twice a night, be available for all emergencies and also write a full report for Matron in the morning. I wrote on all seriously ill patients, pre-op and post-op patients, patients with fevers, new admissions, those for discharge, those in labour, and those delivered during the night. That alone could take two hours. Nurses would bring their ward reports by 4am but there were always last-minute updates such as morning temperatures and changed conditions. At 8am, I would be admitted to Matron's office where I placed the report book in front of her at her desk. Luckily she read it herself but she questioned me all the time. I really don't know how I survived. It was a tremendous challenge and I kept thinking of those great eight-hour shifts with all graduate nurses and wondered what the hell I was doing.

Meanwhile, Madge, a good friend from training days (she was a year behind me), came as staff nurse to the children's ward. She also managed to rent the empty room next to mine at the house. It was nice to have her there though, being on totally different shifts, we rarely saw each other. Robbie became engaged to Peter Butler, a doctor at Barts. She had an engagement party at her flat, which of course I went to and, lo and behold, who was also there but Andy from Vancouver. Andy, an Englishman, was home visiting his parents. It was fun to see him again and to be able to talk about beloved Vancouver. We saw each other a few times and he introduced me to his parents whom I visited several times after he had returned. I enjoyed their hospitality. I had also written to Chris Durling, Bob's sister, and we arranged to meet in London before her departure for Canada. I gave her much advice about trying to get onto ward South 6 at Shaughnessy, the happiest place I knew.

The British Empire Games were being held in Vancouver that year, 1954, too and Chris Chataway was competing in the mile. My beloved cousin by then had—among several high achievements—paced Roger Bannister to the world's first sub-4 minute mile. Chris and Roger met for lunch every year on the anniversary of that ground-breaking achievement.

With my aunt, I had watched him run the 4X1-Mile relay at the White City. Chris had red hair and kept to the back of the pack till the last lap, when suddenly we saw that shock of hair streak ahead. The crowd yelled "Chataway" and my aunt, unable to contain her pride, stood up in the crowd and yelled, "he's mine, he's mine!"

The team set a world record. I'll never forget that mile.

Turning Point

All in all, Vancouver was calling me back. But how? In May of 1955 Anne's Tim was born and that summer the whole family rented a house on the beach front at Lyme Regis. It was a great holiday all together and Bryan christened Tim at Lyme church. In our younger days we had often gone to Lyme for holidays and loved it, so it brought back many good memories. It was there that I received a letter from Andy asking me to return to Vancouver, become engaged, stay in Vancouver for a year, return to the UK to be married, go to Paris for a honeymoon, and return to Vancouver to live. If I agreed, he would meet me in Ottawa and drive me to Vancouver.

How could I pass up this offer?

I did give it a lot of thought and I think my family was slightly against it all. As far as I was concerned, I could see nothing wrong with it. So once more I started to plan. Andy advised me to come in October when he would be in eastern Canada on business. He was a salesman for Reeves paints. I had some friends in Ottawa, who agreed to meet me and put me up when I arrived. I booked a passage on the *SS Homeric*, and Mother and Bryan saw me off in Southampton. As I look back, now that I am a mother, I realize how good that was of Bryan to be with Mother on that momentous day. I was, as ever, being thoroughly selfish, giving no thought to anyone else's feelings but my own.

The *Homeric* was fine and I shared a cabin with a girl my age called Thelma. She was going to Vancouver to stay with an aunt and find work as a secretary. She was terribly seasick and I dragged her up on deck every day to get fresh air. We always seemed to attract a bunch of elderly females who were on a cruise with their priest. Every morning he would recite the rosary and the women would reply with "Holy Mary, Mother of God—Save us." And at that Thelma would retch again. Poor Thelma.

We eventually arrived in Quebec City. Thelma left me her address and caught a train on to Vancouver. I caught a train to Ottawa where my friends met me. They were a dear couple with rather odd grownup sons. I never could quite get the gist of them.

Madge, meanwhile, had left Woolwich and gone to Canada to work at the Sick Children's Hospital in Toronto. She was fearfully homesick so I had asked Andy to pick her up on his way to Ottawa and we could then all spend the weekend together. I could hardly wait to see them both—two of my best friends. It was going to be great. There was no news from either of them on my arrival, but I had no worries. Wonderful to have friends you could rely on 100 percent. I slept soundly that night, so happy to be back in Canada. I had been assured of a position at Shaughnessy on December 1st, so all was set.

The next morning Andy phoned. Excitement rose!

"Where are you? Do you have Madge? When are you coming up?"

Yes, he had Madge and he also had news for me. More excitement.

"Madge and I are engaged."

All I remember was my friend making me sit on a chair.

I was stunned.

A million things raced through my mind. What happened? What was I to do? Why had Madge done this to me?

I just asked if they were going to come up to talk and he agreed. I had a little time to think. I was not going to turn back now. I did not want to work in Ottawa, though my friend tried to persuade me. I did not have the money to either go home or get to Vancouver on my own.

When Andy and Madge arrived, I took them to my room. Madge was in tears, but somehow I managed to say that in ten years' time we would all be laughing at this situation that we had created. I then reminded Andy that he had said he would drive me to Vancouver and that he had better fulfill his promise.

All was agreed. Madge returned to Toronto. I packed my suitcases (luckily no trunk this time—I had learnt my lesson) into the boot of Andy's car and we set off. It snowed. We skidded coming out of Ottawa and Andy panicked. I wondered what on earth I was doing. It kept snowing. The journey was long, physically cold outside, mentally cold inside, and the only song that seemed to be playing on the radio was, "Love and marriage go together like a horse and carriage."

We approached Montana in the deer-hunting season and all the motels were booked solid. In a raging blizzard, we were getting more and more stuck. Eventually we came across a B&B. The woman thought we were a couple. No, no, separate rooms please! I think she vacated her own room for me, and put Andy in with another gent. We were lucky to have found even that.

It must have taken us a week I suppose, but it seemed like a year! As we approached Vancouver, Andy wanted to stop at a friend's house. He had told them he was bringing his fiancée, so as we were welcomed into the house he took them in the kitchen and told them what had happened. Humiliation...

I had previously written to Emil and Elsie Juba telling them of my return to Vancouver, so I asked Andy to drop me off at their address. They had a baby, and lived in one room with a kitchen, sharing a bathroom with a bunch of others. Elsie worked and Emil was going through medical school at UBC. They just threw their arms around me and welcomed me into their home, which could have been a palace. Yes, I could stay for as long as I liked.

I dragged in my suitcases, said goodbye to Andy, thanked him for the ride, and wondered where I was going to sleep. The baby slept in the kitchen, Emil and Elsie slept in a bed in the one room, and I slept on the chesterfield in the same room. To me it was a heavenly oasis. I was with friends—real friends!

Real Friendships

It was November 1955. I immediately went to Shaughnessy, which was within walking distance, and confirmed my position there. Miss Rossiter welcomed me back and told me that I was to be back on South 6. Things were looking brighter. I went to see Mrs. North on South 6, and who should be there but Chris Durling—wow, we were going to be working together.

I then went to look for an apartment. Thelma had said she would like to share one with me. I found one quite close to the hospital and phoned Thelma, who had left for work already. I think her aunt did not want Thelma to move so she never passed on my message. So I had to let that apartment go, as I couldn't afford it on my own. I eventually found a one-bedroom and kitchen, with a shared bathroom, in a house owned by an elderly lady. It was within walking distance from the hospital and in a way I felt it was the best thing. I couldn't rely on any friends, male or female, to share my life ever again.

I soon got myself organized and went back to work in my favourite place. It was just the same, such a happy and well-organized ward. Lots of hard work but a lot of fun too. The great bunch of nurses on the ward included Chris, who had found her way there as I had hoped. Mrs. North and her friend Doreen White took me under their wing and helped me buy my first lot of groceries, transported me about and just generally made sure that I felt right back at home.

And I did. *This* was what I wanted! Not the promise of marriage and all the frills. Funny how things work out.

My family, of course, were amazed at all the happenings, but they were always so positive. I guess they had seen something I had not. I contacted Thelma and she seemed happy enough in her job and digs. I busied myself by joining the choir at the hospital and also making enquiries into joining the Little Theatre, the only theatre group in Vancouver. I had to find a girl who was a window dresser in a large department store. She explained to me that I could join the theatre but that I would have to start at the bottom. Of course I was prepared to do this, and my first job was to do costumes for a play. What a laugh! I had no idea about it, and the leading man, Otto Lowy, lost his Eton collar one night and I found it in the furnace room of this old theatre. Otto later became famous in the art and music world. I was gradually allowed to be on stage, which I loved of course though fitting rehearsals in with shift work was a challenge.

Christmas came and went. New Year was approaching when I got a phone call from Andy. He had obtained my phone number from the hospital and was asking me out for a date. I was floored and reminded him that he was engaged to Madge.

Instead, Thelma and I teamed up with Chris Durling and we went out with a bunch of guys we didn't know. After a party at their house, we all went to Chinatown for grub and the guys drove us back to my place for the rest of the night. I never heard or saw of them again. Wild!

Anne's good friend Hazel had moved to Vancouver and persuaded me to buy skis and go skiing with her. I had great fun on Hollyburn taking skiing lessons from a Scandinavian who pronounced V's as W's. As he taught us to snow plough, sending us one by one down the slope, he would call out "make your *wee* and hold your *wee*." I can still hear Hazel's laugh ringing out over the mountain! We always had to take Max, her black poodle, in the car with us and he barked at every corner we turned. It was a nightmare, especially after eight hours of night duty. Hazel also encouraged me to get my BC driver's license and lent me her car to get it. Hazel was such a secure friend, never interfering but always there when I needed her.

It was the spring of 1956 and Ruth, one of the nurses, was leaving. She shared an apartment in a lovely old house with another nurse whom I had vaguely seen; Ruth suggested that I should take her place since the girl would have to give up the apartment if she had no one to it share with.

No way. I had not the slightest intention of living with anyone and making friends with someone new. Not me! Ruth persisted and persuaded me just to go and have a look at this apartment which in the end under so much pressure I did. This dumpy Germanic girl answered the door and asked me what I wanted. I explained, and she reluctantly showed me the apartment in the top of this huge house. It was magnificent and had a bedroom looking out over the North Shore Mountains.

"This", I said, "I have always wanted."

"This," she replied harshly, "is *my* bedroom."

She then asked if I felt I could live with her. Under no circumstances could I make a friend of her so I asked her the same question.

"Well, you are English and the English talk behind your back, so as long as you don't do that I think I could live with you," she said.

We struck the deal and I moved in. As usual, Hazel was there to help me.

"This dumpy Germanic girl" was named Rita and calmly told me, "I've moved out of that bedroom, you can have it."

Did I detect a slight softness there? Surely not! It really was a great apartment on the very top floor of a lovely old Shaughnessy mansion.

Somehow Rita and I managed to work and live together in a very harmonious way. She grew up in a farming family back east in Ontario and *was* of German extraction. I quickly learnt that Rita had a fearful inferiority complex, which saddened me for she certainly was not in the least inferior. She was far more intelligent than me and a great nurse. She could cook and clean and deal with finances and really taught me a lot. We became the best of friends. Rita had a heart of gold for those she felt needed nurturing and I guess I was one of them.

How lucky I had become once more. Eventually I was introduced to Rita's boyfriend, a guy named Robbie. He was a fun guy, liked his drink which made Rita mad at times. He often made fun of Rita's harshness, her protection from inferiority, which hurt her many times.

RITA AND MYSELF.

JAN • 57

RITA'S ROBBIE

In turn, Rita told me of a chap she had nursed on her ward. He had suffered multiple leg injuries but had moved on to rehab. I think Rita felt sorry for him, as he appeared to have no family. She asked me if I had a boyfriend. I answered her emphatically that I did not, and didn't intend ever to have one, thanks very much! I was too busy with work, the Little Theatre and skiing.

Bob Durling had left the Merchant Navy by now and had come to live in Vancouver with his sister Chris. He was taking a course in land surveying. We met at times but I was beginning to look upon him as a brother. He was just that sort of a person and I had known him a long time.

The nurses on South 6 were a fantastic group. Most of us were single and we were all the same age. All out to have fun. There was one very English girl who got on our wicks at times, but we managed to laugh it off. Mrs. North was aware of all our idiosyncrasies and feelings, but she was always so fair and so honest and expected a high standard of nursing no matter what. Barb Guy and Anne Neill became two very great friends. They shared an apartment and we had fun together. Rita was always fearful of feeling inferior, so didn't mix too readily. Chris Durling of course was also on South 6 and we often went out together too, I lived a very selfish happy life!

Introductions

Rita was determined for me to have a boyfriend. She got in touch with this chap she had nursed and decided we should make a foursome and go to a dog show. I can't say I was that interested in a dog show. It was then, this date, that introduced me to Ken Ramus. He was attentive and quiet, and when Rita asked me afterwards what I thought of him, I replied that I thought he was a homely looking chap. She was upset with me.

Ken had a beat-up old Dodge, which smelt when it rained and, as this was the West Coast that was pretty well all the time. We went out a few times, often as a foursome, and I found him kind, generous and not at all pushy, which attracted me. Ken was working for a cab company, but also was in the Army and was due to go on a training course in Wainwright, Alberta, that summer. He promised to write and left me his address. A few weekends later, Chris asked me if I'd like to go dancing at the YMCA, and I replied that if I received a letter from Ken, then I wouldn't go. If not, then of course I'd love to go dancing. No letter arrived and we went!

I had met some English physios along the way. They worked at the G.F. Strong Rehab Centre where Hazel was in command. One of them, Chris Hill, invited me to go on holiday with her to a dude ranch in the Cariboo. I thought that sounded great. I wrote Ken to tell him, and away Chris and I went. We drove in her Studebaker through the Fraser Canyon to a lodge named Rose Lake near Horsefly in the heart of Cariboo country. It was idyllic. We slept in the lodge and were fed magnificently. It was right on the lake and we rode twice a day through wonderful country. After a few days I received a parcel from Ken. Two cowboy hats! I was thrilled. It was one of the best holidays I had had, and Chris and I seemed to hit it off well.

Ken returned from Wainwright in September. He appeared to have no relations and only a few friends around. Rita had obviously taken him under her wing.

JAN · 57
KEN AND MYSELF

As Ken and I got to know each other better, I learnt a little of his history. Ken had been born in 1925 of English parents in Peru, where his father was a mining engineer in La Oroya. Ken spoke Spanish almost before he spoke English as his mother employed Peruvian servants. At the age of twelve, at a time when further education was non-existent in Peru, Ken's parents had sent him to Shawnigan Lake School, then boys-only, on Vancouver Island. Two of his mother's sisters, Marj and Tid, lived in British Columbia and took turns having Ken for the holidays. Marj lived first at Cowichan Bay and later on Salt Spring Island; Tid lived in New Westminster and later in Kelowna. The move was pretty traumatic for Ken, an only child waited on all his life by native servants and suddenly sent to another country where he knew no one and was pitched into a private boys school. He couldn't even

94

tie his shoelaces when he arrived in this totally foreign environment. Until he turned 18, Ken did not see his parents again.

At graduation, Ken applied to join the army in Canada. Because of his age, he had six months to go before he could enlist. He visited his parents in Peru for the first time since he had left, another shock after his school life in Canada, holidaying with aunts and being expected to fit in with his many cousins.

He returned to Canada in 1944 and joined the army. After initial training he left the country with a division of the Seaforth Highlanders Infantry from Halifax and arrived in England just after D-day. They were immediately sent to France and into the front lines where Ken was shot badly in one leg in March 1945. He returned to England for surgery, followed by plastic surgery and convalescence. While there, he also visited the Millins, a sister of Ken's mother and her surgeon husband plus two daughters, one of them a deaf mute.

When Ken was fully recovered, he was returned to Canada and the army paid for his further education. He already had first year university under his belt, but he had been out and about, seen a bit of life and was not prepared to spend another three years behind a desk. So he chose to take a diesel mechanic's course, which he enjoyed, though his leg did not.

He remained in the army and went on manoeuvres, though of course the war was over. On one of these manoeuvres, he was acting as military police and riding a motorcycle at the end of a convoy when he was rammed in the back, breaking his other leg in several places. Another setback. He was admitted to Shaughnessy hospital where he met Rita. His broken leg was pinned with thirteen screws and his stay in hospital was long.

But Ken had a wonderful positive attitude and a smile that almost stretched from ear to ear, an attraction few could resist. He was then transferred to the convalescing unit called George Derby where he also spent considerable time until finally he was deemed fit to enter the work force. Following his final discharge Ken started to drive for a cab company in Vancouver, had board and room with a family there, and remained a part-time soldier in the army.

Ken and I continued to see a lot of one another and often went out as a foursome. It was a wonderful time. Though I kept my distance to a certain extent, fearful of being hurt once more, I felt this was a man I could trust and love for the rest of time. He was so generous with everything and everyone, so true with no "side" to him. He lived life as it came and rolled with the punches.

My first hesitation, however, came on November 11th, 1956 when Ken had attended Remembrance Day parade. I had a day off and was looking forward to spending the rest of the day together. Not so! He rang me several times during the day saying they were "obliged" to visit the army messes to "celebrate!" I had never thought of November 11th as a celebration—I thought it was to remember the dead. However I was learning fast and by 9pm Ken arrived at the apartment slightly worse for wear, asking only for a glass of milk!

My second hesitation came when Ken proposed to me. Rita asked me what had been my reply. I told her, as I had told him, that he would have to do a different job, as I couldn't write home and tell them I was marrying a cab driver. She was horrified and told me in no uncertain terms, "Doreen, it is not what a man does, it is what a man *is* that counts."

I am ashamed to say that that had never entered my head.

We spent a wonderful Christmas all together at the apartment. Ken and I became engaged on December 29th, 1956. I phoned home and told the family, and we also made a tape recording. Rodney had been out that fall and met Ken and had told the family that he "approved." That was a big milestone.

I had made two very great friends, Bent and Tonny Mortenson, who lived in an apartment underneath us. They were Danish and had just produced a daughter, Marianne. They asked Ken and me whether, if we were to get married, we would we be godparents to Marianne. We accepted and so began another great set of friends.

KEN.

Barb Guy and Jack Nicholson, an intern at Shaughnessy, were to be married in Kelowna in February and we were all invited to the wedding. Ken said he would ask his aunt in Kelowna to find us a motel for the weekend. And so we stayed at the Beacon Beach, or Brothel as we nicknamed it though a purer weekend you couldn't ask for. Sitting in the church waiting for Barb suddenly gave me cold feet; I thought I just couldn't deal with all this for myself. But it was a great wedding, and Anne Neill was the maid of honour. The next day Ken's aunt invited him and me to lunch. I dreaded it, feeling more and more that this whole deal was not for me. I imagined his aunt to be a little old woman, living behind a picket fence in a little old house. No, I must break the whole thing off!

We arrived at 637 Burne Avenue. There it was, picket fence and all! Ken's aunt was tall with a wonderful kind face but not in the least bit gushy or how I had imagined her. As she stood in the doorway, I noticed behind her a dining room table laid in exactly the same way my mother would have laid it. I started to weaken. As we talked I saw where Ken's roots were. If this woman—Tid—was his mother's sister and had looked after Ken during his school holidays, I could see why he was the man he was and all my doubts faded. She became my second mother!

I should perhaps relate that Madge came out to Vancouver for a while, but we didn't really see much of one another. Andy was transferred to Toronto and they were married in 1956 in England, honeymooned in Paris (as had been his original plans), and returned to the suburbs of Toronto to live. I felt sad at our estrangement, yet Madge seemed to think that nothing was amiss. She never wrote but did phone me one day asking me to be godmother to her second child, Anne. The christening was the next day so I felt obliged to accept. I wanted to remain friends, yet I felt she was so distant.

Weddings

Rita and Robbie were married in June of that year, 1957. It was of course perfection. Her mother, brother and sister-in-law came from Ontario and we all bunked down in the apartment. I was maid of honour and Ken was best man. It was all pretty stressful as Rita was so afraid of letting some side down. There had been so many ups and downs in their relationship, partly due to drink, that when the parson finally pronounced them man and wife, I nearly collapsed with relief.

Ken had received an army compensation package, so we were able to buy a decent car and put a down payment on a house in the university area of Vancouver. It was a dear little house with two bedrooms, a sawdust furnace and a dirt floor in the basement. I loved it.

The house needed a lot of work but we attacked it with full force. I moved in and we bought odd bits of second-hand furniture. We sanded and varnished floors, painted and really made a difference to the place. We set our wedding date for the 30th of August. Mother was accompanying Anne and Co. out to New York where Rodney had got a job with GE in Schenectady and arranged it so that she could "give me away" at the wedding. We wrote to Ken's mother, Foncy, and asked her for a list of people she would like to invite to the wedding. I was nonplussed! The list was enormous. When I asked Ken who all these people were, he explained that they were all relations. And I had thought he was all alone in this world. Foncy accepted our invitation but Ray, Ken's father, did not, which was a pity.

It was fun getting everything organized for our mothers' arrivals and for the wedding. Near our house was St. Helen's Church where we had attended, and liked the parson, Whin Robinson. All was duly arranged there. We had chosen a lovely old restaurant by the university with a great view of the sea for our reception. I was still at work of course and Ken was now full-time in the army as a military policeman. Rita insisted on me seeing a gynaecologist and getting fitted with a diaphragm as a method of birth control. All new to me. What a palaver!

On arrival Mother stayed in the house with me. Foncy stayed at the Grosvenor Hotel with her sisters, Tid and Marj.

MOTHER'S ARRIVAL.

The night before the wedding Foncy entertained the whole wedding party and us at a dinner at the Georgia hotel. It was a great night. Next morning Tid, Marj and Foncy converged on our house and chatted with Mother. Through all their talk we discovered that Marj's daughter, Nonie, went to a school on Vancouver Island and its headmistress had once been a parishioner of Father's in Weymouth, and had sought his advice about coming to Canada to form a British type of girls' boarding school! This of course made a great link between the women. After they left, Mother confided in me, as only Mother would: "They are all out of the same drawer as us, dear!" It was so important to Mother, I realized, and now I see exactly what she meant.

A little Chinese lady, who was incredible, made my dress. It was so beautiful! Robbie sent me her veil to wear which really thrilled me. Rita was my maid of honour and Thelma was my bridesmaid; Mother gave me away.

It was a wonderful wedding with lots of music and one hundred people attended. Mother sat with Hazel. Bob Durling drove us to the church and Chris's new husband, Bob Tween, recorded the whole service. Ernie Colter sang "The Lord's Prayer" and Whin was great. The reception went well and before we left we had to say a sad farewell to Foncy who was returning to Peru. I don't really know how Ken felt. He had told me earlier that Tid had become more of a mother to him than Foncy. Sad for both of them. Hazel took care of Mother, and eventually drove her to Kelowna to stay with Tid.

Ken and I left for our honeymoon to the Oregon coast, spending our first night in Bellingham. The ritual of the diaphragm was quite something but I managed it and, as Mother had told me, my first wedding night was perfect!

We spent a great honeymoon travelling down the Oregon coast and inland as far as Crater Lake. However I had developed a fearful sore throat with a high fever. As we headed home, I began to feel worse and worse. We arrived at Tid's in Kelowna and she immediately called a doctor who gave me huge antibiotic capsules. I could hardly swallow. Mother was there, which was great, as I felt so awful. In the end we decided to head back to Vancouver and took Mother with us. When I got home a doctor friend came and gave me a shot of penicillin. That really helped and I soon recovered. Mother stayed for a little while longer and then returned to Anne in New York. I had so appreciated Mother being with me. She had attended all the wedding showers, so she had met many of my friends. It must have been a strange whirl for her.

AUGUST 30th 1957

That first Christmas I had to work, but Ken gathered in all the stray men that were around— Bob Durling, Bob Tween, Robbie, and Frank, an Australian who lived with us for a while—and they had a good Christmas dinner. Our New Year's Eve was great as we hosted it at our house and had all our good friends who had become really like family to us: Bob Durling and girlfriend Jackie Snow, who worked on South 6, Chris and Bob Tween, Rita and Robbie, Bent and Tonny Mortenson, and Frank. We found this punch recipe and everyone brought some of the ingredients. It was so successful that we all made it every year. It became a tradition.

Married Life

The year 1958 saw many changes. Life seemed to move along smoothly at first. I came to know Ken's cousin Tony Griffin, Tid's son, who stayed with us on his way to and from Hawaii. Tony had attended our wedding. He was a lot of fun but wore at least two shirts a day, all of which needed washing and ironing. We had purchased a blue roan Cocker Spaniel and, since he was black and white, we called him Whiskey. He was a great dog.

In the summer of that year I began to run a very high fever and was hospitalised in the University Hospital. Doctor Waldie looked after me and after several tests announced that I was pregnant! Then it hit, and for the next three months I was sick, every day, all day, and felt like death. I continued to work the best I could. Another nurse on the ward, Mary McIvor, was pregnant too, but she was fine. An occupational therapist, Christine Keene, was also "that way" and she was as fit as a fiddle. The three of us would get together and discuss our fate.

I left Shaughnessy in October. Mother decided to give up her house and move into The Matron's College in Salisbury Close, which were little self-contained houses under one roof that were provided for widows and orphans of clergy. I went home to England that month to help her move. I was feeling much better; it was great to see Mother settled again within easy access of shops and the Cathedral. Unfortunately I missed the wedding of Bob Durling and Jackie Snow, who were married that month in St. Helen's Church.

When I returned, the axe had fallen on the army. They were cut back drastically, so Ken was unemployed. I had given up work and was seven months pregnant. What to do? Bob Durling was also unemployed, and he and Ken went to pick up their Unemployment Insurance cheques together every two weeks. Ken was able to do a lot around the house, but we had no income. We advertised at the university to see if we could take in a boarder, and at once this tall young man arrived at our door. It was the beginning of a lasting friendship. Bruce Grant was fresh out of school trying to go through university. He lived on Salt Spring Island, where Ken's aunt Marj and his uncle Bevill had a guesthouse. Bruce, who paid us 75 dollars a month for full board and room, was a delight to have with us in the house.

We bought a second-hand buggy and Ken and Bruce painted it all up in a brilliant blue while Christine Keene re-upholstered the inside. It was gorgeous and just what I wanted as it had a "well" to put the shopping in. We bought a second-hand crib and playpen, and really started to get excited about extending our family.

Christmas of 1958 was spent on Salt Spring with Marj and Bevill and others at "Aclands". This rather Japanese-looking house was right on the sea at the mouth of the Booth Bay Canal. It was idyllic, and Marj and Bevill were so great. I loved them both dearly. Unfortunately, Whiskey ate one of Bevill's bantams, but it all seemed par for the course to Bevill. New Year's was spent in the usual fashion at our house, with the usual conglomerate of friends including Bruce.

Motherhood

January 1959, the 19th, I went into labour and was admitted into St. Vincent's Hospital. There I laboured for three days before they finally gave me a spinal anaesthetic and delivered me, with forceps, of our first gorgeous daughter, Helen Margaret! She weighed some six pounds and had a smattering of reddish hair. We were so thrilled; all the memory of the agony she had caused disappeared. I was a mother—how incredible! I went home after a week in hospital; Bruce was so helpful to Ken and just fitted in as part of our family. Mary, Christine and I had all been to prenatal classes and though the three of us were due at the same time, I was the first one to have the baby.

Three weeks later I was smitten with the most ghastly chest pain, something I had never experienced. It was so agonizing that I could hardly nurse our lovely baby. What was happening? Ken sent for Dr. Waldie, who eventually came and called in a doctor I knew from Shaughnessy. He diagnosed an acute gall bladder attack and whisked me straight back into St Vincent's. Helen was my only concern but it seemed she was no concern of theirs. They immediately stuck up an IV and gave me a shot of Demerol. Meanwhile, Ken and Bruce were literally left holding the baby.

Chris Tween was pregnant and had left Shaughnessy; she offered to look after Helen and put her onto the bottle. What would I have done without her? Ken was doing some guard-duty job at all hours, also trying to cope with Bruce and meals and washing. After about a week, all settled down and I came home. I heard then that the other babies had been born: Mary had a boy, Denis and Christine had a girl, too easily, Amanda. The Keenes and us became very good friends, and have remained so.

Ken and I struggled on financially. We decided that he would always deal with the money and pay the bills. However Ken was not the best at this and we were sinking deeper and deeper in debt.

One day I had written to Mother and found that I did not have enough money to buy a stamp to mail the letter. This was rock bottom. What were we to do? We were literally living on Bruce's money, and that only covered food. Ken was dealing with this guard-duty job, which entailed a list of houses all over Vancouver that needed to be checked for security. It paid very little; in fact sometimes I wondered really if we broke even after paying for gas.

Helen was christened at St. Helen's.

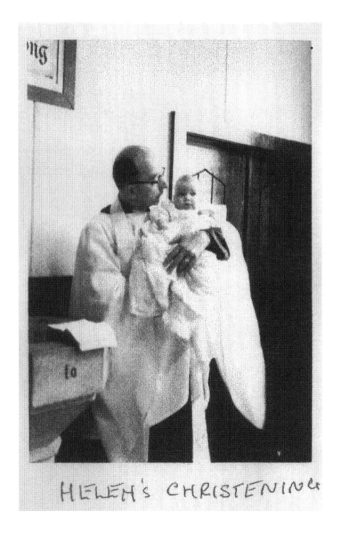

HELEN'S CHRISTENING

Shawnigan Lake

March of 1959 saw a turn of events. Nonie Guthrie, the daughter of Marj and Bevill, had been asked to reopen Strathcona Lodge School, the school that Minna Gildea had formed when she came from Weymouth. Nonie got in touch with us and asked Ken if he would be in charge of all the maintenance of the school and if I would be the school matron. Well, it seemed an answer to prayer. We couldn't refuse. First we had to sell the house, which was sad.

We went over to Vancouver Island to Shawnigan Lake to see Nonie and the school.

STRATHCONA.

The vast old building, originally a Canadian Pacific Railway hotel, overlooked the lake. On the other side was the boys' school that Ken had attended. Nonie suggested that we live on the dormitory floor where we would have two rooms. I stuck out against this. We were a family and we needed to live as a family in our own space. We looked around for a house and found one down the road. The owner had just died and her niece was ready to sell the home for 7,000 dollars. It was a done deal. We sold our Vancouver house for the same price as we had paid for it (minus mortgage payments).

Our new house was old and had only been a summer cottage. It had been raised so that it consisted of a small dining room, a sitting room with oil heater, a kitchen with wood stove, an outhouse with washing sinks, and a tree that held up the bathroom upstairs. The second floor consisted of one huge communal bedroom with a light bulb hanging from a high ceiling. If you could find its string in the dark, the bulb would shed light over all. There was a balcony off this room and also the bathroom, which was a plus. The back of the house led to the railway tracks and was covered in huge trees. The front was full of blackberry bushes and not much else. It faced the road.

We rented a truck and, with the help of all our friends, packed everything up. Bruce and Robbie came with us to help at the other end. It was really a bit traumatic for me, leaving behind good friends and establishing ourselves on Vancouver Island in totally new jobs, also working for relations. However, this was far better, I kept saying, than going deeper into debt.

We soon got ourselves settled in. Ken attacked the swath of trees at the back, felling them and cutting them up for firewood for our woodstove. We fixed up our old washing machine in the outhouse and generally made up our home again. University had finished and Bruce stayed with us on and off, helping Ken make the upstairs more habitable. It was all quite a revelation as between the walls were cedar boughs to keep out the moths. They were tinder dry and would have been dandy fuel if the house had caught fire. Ken and Bruce installed insulation, put up partitions to make three bedrooms, and pushed out the wall to the balcony and enclosed it, making a huge master bedroom.

There was much to be done at the school before it opened in September. Ken was fully occupied and I became more and more aware that I was not only to be matron but also housekeeper, for which I was totally unprepared. The cooks, who were German, had a small baby boy the same age as Helen. Helen came to work with us every day. I had found an old crib, which we dillied up and put in the dispensary. When not asleep in this, Helen was either outside in the buggy or in a playpen I had also found. She was no trouble at all and Whiskey always was near Helen as if to protect her. What a dog! We had found rats in our house ceiling so we also acquired a cat. He was pure white so we called him Soda.

Nonie ran the school in a much more relaxed way than English boarding schools were, something I found difficult to deal with at first. However, bit by bit I came to understand my role and how to deal with it. Robin Garland came from England and was yet another of Ken's relations. Her grandmother, Norah, was another of Foncy's sisters and lived in Scotland. There was another teacher from England, Norah Arthurs, so I soon felt more at home with everyone. The girls were a different bunch—the majority had been sent to Strathcona because of difficulties at home. One became pregnant right off the bat and of course had to go home. There was also "Minty", Nonie's husband. He was much older than Nonie, but a dear, and really good with everyone.

In October of 1959 Ken was dismantling an old fire escape when the whole thing pulled out from the wall and he fell three storeys, luckily onto a pile of cordwood. He broke both his feet and suffered a huge gash across his forehead. He was transported to hospital where he stayed for a few days, and returned with both feet in plaster. He tried to work with plastic bags over his feet, but the plasters became soggy too often and he finally had to give up. Luckily Bruce was around and took over his job until Ken could tackle it again. That was a tough month, as we just had to live on my wage, which was not much.

Helen's first Christmas was memorable. I have never seen a child receive so many gifts. It was quite overwhelming. This Christmas was also my full introduction to many of Ken's relatives. After school was finished I had to prepare all the dormitory floor rooms for the arrival of "the family." I would have to include a family tree because they are too numerous to write them all down. At least thirty of us sat down to Christmas dinner that night. Tony had decorated the table, which seated us all on the outside of a square. I had never seen anything like it. At the appointed time, everyone descended the wide staircase and entered the dining room two by two, a lady on the arm of a gent. We women were all in evening dress and the gents in tuxedos. Helen was safely tucked up in her crib in the dispensary, with Whiskey keeping guard outside the door. I suddenly felt desperately homesick for my own dear family. I really didn't know these people, and all this pomp and circumstance seemed so overwhelming. It was so different. Even though everyone seemed pleased to meet me, I felt very much on the outside. After dinner we played games upstairs in the huge common room, which eased things a bit, but I was glad to get home to our own little abode.

1960 saw more problems. We continued with our work routine but I could see that Ken and Nonie were beginning to cross swords. Ken did things in his own way and was too stubborn to be subservient to his female cousin. Soon the axe fell and Nonie told him he must look for something else at the end of the summer term. It was a blow but, if worse came to worst, I could go back to nursing in Duncan and he could look after Helen. He at once started putting feelers out for a different job; perhaps we should move to Victoria or go back to Vancouver, although living in cities had become more expensive.

Then another axe fell. I was becoming increasingly sick and felt like death. Oh dear God, I must be pregnant. I didn't want Nonie to know as I thought then she would feel obligated to keep Ken on and I didn't want any handouts. The Matron at the boys' school came to my rescue and every ten days she "shot" me with vitamin B, which cut down the nausea and enabled me to continue working. In the end Nonie caught on and said that Ken could stay on until he found something else. Mother came out that summer; it was so wonderful to have her. Robin took Helen, Raisins as she called her, for a few days and Ken and I took Mother on a small tour of the Island. It was so good to have a break. Ken took holidays at this time and scoured the job market, unsuccessfully.

Christine and Denis with Amanda would come over at weekends often, which was a welcome relief from the stress we were going through. We played endless games of Monopoly which was always fun. There was no other social life except for the fact that I joined the Shawnigan Players and got involved in a play, which I loved.

Philippa Keene was born that November and they all came over at Christmas time. I felt better about the family. I had met many of them again that year, and visited Marj and Bevill several times on Salt Spring. Marj was so kind to us all. She knew the situation, never took sides and was always a tower of strength to us. I began to feel part of Ken's family and not just an employee of Strathcona.

1961 was an eventful year. I worked till the end of January and started to prepare for the birth of our second child. I was called to the school one night when I was elbow deep in cleaning the kitchen stove. A girl had fallen and twisted her knee badly—would I come at once? I didn't change, just washed my hands and flew up to the school. Robin met me and ushered me up to the common room where the girl was supposed to be lying. All seemed so quiet. Robin opened the door and there was the whole school gathered.

No injured knee, just a baby shower for me! I was overwhelmed and felt so guilty that the parents, who had paid so much for their girls' education, should have to fork out more for a gift for me. However I was really grateful for everything and especially the thought behind it all.

Mother Act

In the whirl of working while trying to understand "motherhood", I suppose my passion for portraying another—better—character on stage had taken over. I auditioned for a role in a play with the Shawnigan Players. Happily rehearsing, I suddenly caught on that my second child would be born around the time of the production. Oh dear.

The play continued rehearsals. I went into labour. On February 13th in the early morning Ken took me to King's Daughters Hospital. I was *not* having a child on Valentine's Day so I did my damndest to push that baby out. Bruce arrived at 11.45pm.

In my franticness to have this baby, I heard one of the nurses say, "This one's a good actress." I was furious and told her in no uncertain terms that I was not acting. The nurse apologized and cleared her statement by saying she had seen me in a play in Duncan.

Once the baby had been deemed fit for his father to view him through the nursery window, Ken was right there together with our lodger, Sam, who was from Jamaica. The nurse picked up a "brown" baby. Ken was frantic, shouting through the window "R-A-M-U-S." All was duly righted but not until the Shawnigan policeman, viewing his own baby, had taken in all the shenanigans.

Later as I wheeled Bruce along in his pram through the village, the policeman looked in at the baby. He smiled and said, "My, that's a pretty good bleach job!"

Back to the play! One dress rehearsal left! On to the stage!

I was nursing Bruce, so I padded myself up well and made the cast promise not to mention drinks of any kind lest my milk supply kicked in at the wrong moment. All was well when I returned home to a hungry baby—what a relief.

Meanwhile, friends had taken Helen for a week so I was able to get back to normal. I no longer worked at the school, thankfully.

Caring for my two great children, my husband, and the lodger was quite the eye-opener. I loved it, if only we could have had a little more money.

Our friends, the Keenes, with their newborns, often visited from Vancouver. It was a time of a completely different life, discussing our children, trying to understand this weird thing that had happened to us. We were, I suppose, all elderly parents trying to outdo one another.

BRUCE'S CHRISTENING.

Helen was wonderful, helping me with Bruce. She seemed to understand everything so I almost let her "take over". Now we were living only on Ken's paltry wage of 200 dollars, plus Sam's meagre board and room per month. Had Helen caught on to this? Only by a process of osmosis, as far as I could determine. One day, sitting with Sam as he shovelled vast amounts of sugar into his coffee, Helen gazed at the cup and remarked, "That's enough Sam, sugar costs pennies!"

In 1962, at the age of 36, I wondered if was entering menopause. Whatever! The public health nurse often popped in for a cuppa and I told her my thoughts. She quickly told me that my predicament was *not* menopause but another pregnancy. I was not vomiting as I had done with Helen and Bruce. Slow as I was to catch on to all these changes, I looked forward to the arrival of Sarah in October of that year. My wonderful friend Rita came to stay with us and helped me through a frantic time.

SARAH's BIRTH.

With three small ones, two lodgers (Big Bruce, as we called him after little Bruce was born, had joined us again) and Ken not happy in his job, we were becoming disillusioned with life. Where was this going? Absolutely nowhere.

In December of that year we received a phone call from our good friend Bent Mortensen, saying they had moved to Squamish where he was overseeing the building of the sawmill. Bent thought Ken could apply for a job there. We left Helen and Bruce with friends, took Sarah with us and headed straight for Squamish.

New Beginning

What was this job Ken could apply for? Scow spotter. Whatever it was, Ken was game. He applied, feeling it was our only hope. We quickly looked around Squamish and hopped on the ferry back to Shawnigan. Helen, Bruce, Whiskey and Soda were happy to be together again.

The school was putting on a Christmas play. Would I consider letting Sarah be the Baby Jesus? No problem. The night of the production I sat backstage with my Sarah waiting for her cue to be "born". She had other ideas. Long before her appropriate debut on stage, Sarah started screaming—colic. Nothing pacified her. So Baby Jesus was born slightly premature. As usual, I felt the blame was on my shoulders.

Next came the highly anticipated phone call, accepting Ken's application as a scow spotter. Our lives were about to change. Were we prepared for this mammoth upheaval? Though the three years at Shawnigan Lake had financially helpful, Ken did not like working for his cousin. Nonie, in turn, was struggling with her first real job of forming and running the school. She was the boss but Ken had his ideas and I had learnt quickly that it was unwise to cross Ken.

Ken left at once for Squamish, leaving Big Bruce to fill his shoes at the school. Ken was fulltime working a crane, loading lumber onto scows, which transported it all to mills in Vancouver. When off duty, he scoured Squamish for a house for us. He was staying with Bent and Tonny, sleeping in their furnace room. There were no houses to rent. Ken was determined for us all to be together so he found a house in North Vancouver just off Capilano bridge. With much help from friends, trucks were loaded.

We left in our Austin station wagon packed to the gunnels, plus the three children and the two pets. On to the ferry car deck, where at once Bruce and Helen wanted out. Luckily Sarah was in a carrycot. Doors opened. Out went Whiskey and Soda. Ken offered to look after the kids while I ran through the car deck yelling, "Whiskeee, Sodah."

A kind gentleman opening his trunk stopped me, saying, "I have some vodka, would that help?" What on earth was he talking about? All I wanted was my dog and cat.

We arrived, at last, on the mainland and quickly settled ourselves in our North Vancouver home. Meanwhile Ken kept desperately looking for a home to rent in Squamish to get rid of his hour-and-a-half commute.

Our North Vancouver house had a wood furnace, which Ken stoked before leaving for work. We had two bedrooms but Sarah was still in a crib in our room. At some point Helen and Bruce had their tonsils out in Lions Gate Hospital. I hated that but knew it was for the best. One was not welcome to sit with them at any time. In any case, I had Sarah to look after. All went well.

We were only in this house for about three months when Ken found one to rent in Brackendale, an area of Squamish. More help with friends and trucks. As we drove into the carport, our new neighbour looked at us all, plus dog and cat, and yelled over her prized dahlias, "Don't let any of that lot in my yard!" Lovely welcome but we did become the best of friends eventually.

The Brackendale house was a three-bedroom rancher. Oh joy! But our lodgers, Big Bruce and Sam, descended on us so we were back to two rooms again. The yard was great for the two eldest to play in every morning while Sarah slept in her buggy outside.

After about three weeks, Ken came down with severe sinusitis and, because of the sawdust at the mill, had to stay home. Money? Forever tight and on my mind. I phoned the Squamish hospital and told them I would be willing to work casual. Ken could look after the kids. I was called the next day.

What a hospital. More experience. This twenty five-bed hospital took in everything. Motor vehicle accidents, heart attacks, maternity—you name it, it all came through the door with no notice and no doctors present. Two or three registered nurses were on the day shift, from 7am to 3.30pm, while a registered nurse with one practical nurse had the rest of the 24 hours. It could be chaotic, but we also had time for a laugh or two. Though often terrified, I loved it. I worked every day for a week until Ken was well enough to go back to work.

Squamish was definitely going to be our home. So we started looking for a lot to build a house. The Army was being generous and, together with developer Pat Goode, they arranged for veterans to build on half-acre lots in Garibaldi Highlands. We decided to aim for a lot at the top of the Highlands, up Skyline Drive as far as it went, turning left on a track eventually called Braemar and left again on a track called Ayr Drive. A couple of houses were being built here so we went along this track as far as the bush would let us, opposite what is now Argyle Crescent.

Pat Goode met us, waxing enthusiastically over this lot with a beautiful view. We saw nothing but trees. However we felt this was where we could settle—in the heart of bush country. The lot was not half an acre but Pat didn't worry: nothing beyond this had been surveyed so he just added on a bit to make up. No problem. The Veterans' Land Act accepted our mortgage and the man down the road, Al Werger, was a builder so we were all set.

Bit by bit the lot was cleared enough to start the house in 1963.

We chose a design and away Al Werger went. We could tell he was a brilliant builder, leaving nothing to chance. After the final inspection by VLA, we were told that even a bulldozer would have a hard time knocking it down.

In 1964 we moved in, but that first night I had to work. Never mind. Here was our home where we could become a settled family again. We couldn't have been happier. The hospital kept calling but I had to decline for want of a daytime babysitter. After a while, Mrs. Applin Flouch, the hospital administrator's wife, offered to take our three kids for a day shift. So, at the crack of dawn, I got the children up, dressed, fed and into the car with bottles, baby food, diapers and playpen. Luckily the Applin Flouch family lived next to the hospital and so I left the kids there till I picked them up at 3.30pm for home, supper and bed.

Helen, then five years old, Bruce, three, and Sarah, 15 months, were so good, never making a fuss.

I belonged to the Anglican Church where dear Ruth Fenton roped me in to teach Sunday school. Ruth's sister, Betty, ran a kindergarten so I enrolled Helen. She began to meet friends and was able to occupy her busy mind and hands. Helen became my right hand, always caring for the other two, something for which I never really showed my appreciation. It just became so natural and I should have given her so much more praise and thanks.

I gradually got the hang of Squamish. At first I felt unwelcomed. Until the road to Vancouver had been opened just a few years earlier in 1959, the only access to the town had been by boat. This created the sense of a closed-in community. Looking back I can imagine how this small logging town felt towards outsiders invading their space and taking their employment. However, slowly our family began to feel accepted, partly, I think, because I became known at the hospital and Ken at the mill and the Lions Club. We *were* giving of ourselves to the community. Houses were being built on Ayr Drive, and Bruce became friendly with Mauro Vescera whose Italian parents lived just down the road. This turned into a lasting friendship. Most of us on Ayr Drive were new so it became a community of its own and we all knew each other.

However things tend not to stand still. The lot next door was cleared for a house built for a family known vaguely by Ken's family. Mervyn Barrington Foote had opened up a men's clothing store in Squamish. It meant little to me; in fact, I thought a menswear store was a bit off as all men wore logging outfits. Then all became clear and the connection made.

In 1966 the Footes moved in next door. Lorraine and Merv had four children—Randy, Norm, Stephen, and Lori. Lori and our Sarah, then both four years old, became inseparable and have remained so to this day.

ON OUR LOT IN
GARIBALDI HIGHLANDS

History of the Foote Path

After the Foote family moved in next door, the Foote Path became a physical entity. Our kids had fun together. Stephen was a tease to the girls. Norm, quiet looking for all opportunities to come his way, teamed up with Little Bruce as they got older, with many a rendezvous outside our basement back door. Norm was keen to learn the piano, and when our doors were locked he would squeeze through the pet door to practice in our basement. Randy, the Foote's eldest, was distant, probably because he felt far above these younger "rang-a tang" kids. At some stage Randy grew an Afro and lived in a disused school bus. Later he became the "Bossy Banker." Our Helen, at seven years old, seemed to be in charge of everyone, or else decided to disown the lot. Stephen was a terrible tease but oh so full of life and spunk. When he grew up Stephen worked at the mill. One day he fell off a ladder and broke his back, which left him a paraplegic. This never stopped him. One night, while out partying with a pal who was driving him home, their car slammed into a power pole ejecting and killing Stephen. We were all devastated. He left behind a small son whom the Foote family has always supported.

Lorraine and I became the best of friends, though were never in each other's pockets. We celebrated any little joy that came into our lives as well as the big moments like weddings and births. We also shared deeply the many pitfalls that occur in so many families. Merv was fulltime at the store but always ready to be of help, taking the kids to the PNE summer fair in Vancouver, which Ken and I never did. The Footes also included Sarah in many of their holidays.

The Foote Path was worn thin, carrying endless Foote and Ramus feet traversing it. Beside it, I planted a nut tree where I thought Lorraine and I could sit and drink tea, and discuss our families, which we had become so familiar with on both sides. We poured out our worries and laughed at so many pleasures we had seeing our children growing up and going their very different ways.

Tragedy hit again—didn't we expect something else would mar our lives? Lorraine showed me the lump in her neck. That then was the beginning of the end. Giving the eulogy at Lorraine's funeral, I nearly lost it when I saw Mandy, her granddaughter, sitting in the front with her baby, knowing how much Lorraine had meant to her and to so many, including myself.

After Lorraine died, we used the Foote path once more to transport "Meals on Feete" to Merv. When both Merv and Lorraine had left us, the house was sold, and a fence built—the end of the physical Foote Path. Nothing in this world, I hope, will ever erase the bond that was created by the physical Foote Path. As far as I am concerned, it lives on through the generations that have come after. May that bond never be broken.

Squamish – The Early Years

In those early years my life seemed a complete whirl. The children were growing up; the house needed finishing, with the basement made liveable for a fourth bedroom, play area and laundry. The garden needed to be created. Everywhere was bush. Little Bruce by then was four and of course was warned regarding sharp tools such as axes. Nevertheless, at four, one must try everything. Next I knew were voices in the basement where Helen had Bruce in her command, mopping up a cut on his head from trying out the forbidden axe. Helen started school in September of 1965 and even there seemed in command of many practical happenings.

Meanwhile I worked at the hospital on eight-hour nights, returning home around 6.30am so that Ken could get to work, the children breakfasted and Helen off to school. Bruce and Sarah seemed to occupy themselves with newfound friends, though I put both kids down to rest in the afternoon so that I could catch a bit of shut-eye before the next night shift. When I look back, I am sure I was not a good mother, but I loved my kids, my home and my work. Nursing was so satisfying. It was always a challenge as one was so alone in it all.

One night I had a call from Woodfibre, a town across the Howe Sound, saying they had an unconscious female they were shipping over. I phoned the doctor to alert him, but he seemed disinterested, saying he was with another doctor helping him get a skunk out of his sitting room. Another call came in from the ferry, saying the female was a teenager who was inebriated. Again, I alerted the doctor on call. His reply was quick. "Ask her what she has been drinking, if it's rum, pump her out and we'll have a party." Needless to say, none of this happened—doctors could always be relied upon when necessary. Those were the unexpected turns we had to deal with. We kept the girl overnight, allowing her to overcome her alcohol binge and put her back on the ferry.

There were many other more dramatic instances of course. In such a small hospital, everything came through the doors. The highway stretched to Whistler, which was developing quickly. Road accidents were common, as were railway accidents. Heart conditions kept us on our toes, as did maternity cases. As I was the only trained midwife, it was always my job to step in for obstetric cases and was often called in to deal with these.

However there were always moments when a sense of humour saved the day. The hospital's not-so-silent silent waiter brought meals up from the kitchen in the basement to the nurses' station. If you were lucky it would also take a specimen down with a request for someone to deliver it to the lab. Why not? Saved the stairs.

A gynaecologist was visiting from Vancouver to help one of our doctors do some surgery. As I walked past the doctors' changing room, I spied their pants slung over the extra bed in there. Unable to resist, I found a needle and thread, and sewed up their pants. Surgery over, we all descended to the dining room for coffee. The doctors were dressed properly. Nothing was said. I was somewhat disappointed at their lack of humour.

At the end of my shift, I picked up my purse and left to do some grocery shopping. My purse felt unusually heavy. Bent on shopping and getting home to cook supper and pick up the pieces of home life, I arrived at the cashier with a line of shoppers behind me. I opened my purse to pay when two metal vaginal specula fell out in front of the cashier. I was mortified! I quickly picked them up and deposited them with my shopping, anxious to leave others wondering what I was going to do with my two unwanted "purchases".

Needless to say, I "thanked" those two doctors the next time for their gifts.

In my mind, life was a continuous whirl. Supper was always a meal where we sat down to the table, ate what was put in front of us, and viewed the day. Ken dished out the supper and was strict over eating all that was on our plates, which created much tension at times with the children, especially Bruce. Both Ken and I, having lived through the war, thought nothing of the need for clean plates but had to be cautioned about the need for a little leeway.

KEN AND MYSELF   HOME

At the weekends, if I was not working, we tried to spend more time with the children as opposed to the property. We took them up to Whistler, which was then only Creekside, and let the kids experience skiing. There was just a rope tow but Helen and Bruce soon caught on and enjoyed themselves. At first Sarah learned standing on the back of my skis. Ken did not attempt this sport, as his knees were too valuable for work.

Gradually all three loved skiing. I gave it up, so we could buy Sarah a pair of skis. Soon Rainbow opened up beyond Whistler and offered ski lessons. Ken and I sat in the coffee room at the bottom of the slope, watching the progress (or lack thereof), chatting, planning, and sometimes nodding off. We thought about buying a lot in Whistler, but a cabin had to be built within a year of purchasing. We felt it would all be a bit too much to tackle. As winters slowly moved into spring, horseback riding was next on the agenda. There was a stable in Paradise Valley, just a 30-minute drive, where we could rent horses. Once more the kids loved it and we enjoyed our Saturdays up there.

At first I taught Sunday school and tried to instil church into the family. Dressing in "good clothes" for the event soon became a chore, though the kids and Ken went along with my "whim" for quite a few years. Church had always been a source of strength to me but it gradually became irrelevant to this crazy life of raising a family and being a good mother and wife. Perhaps I should have stuck closer to it!

Our summer holidays were spent in the Okanagan with Tid, Ken's aunt. She was so good to us all, never raising the money side of things to Ken and even hiring a baby sitter to give me a bit of a break. We loved her and later I was able to nurse Tid at the end of her life in my home.

Howe Sound Drama Club

Garibaldi Highlands was growing rapidly with mostly new families like us. House parties were the norm. One such house party Ken and I attended consisted of eight couples. All were relative strangers to us. I looked around and suddenly thought, "These people could act." At once I handed round a paper plate, asked each one to donate two dollars. With 32 dollars, I intended to start a drama club. Why on earth, Doreen, when you have enough on your plate already? When the urge is there, it needs to be obeyed!

After a few setbacks I bought the script for *Aladdin*. The group, about twelve of us, rehearsed in basements. Gradually it all came together and we performed in Mamquam School in 1966 together with a school choir and band. Just *one* night! What was I thinking?

Many thespians came on board, performing as many as three plays a year. Rehearsal and performing venues were hard to come by but we all struggled through and were deemed the arrival of the first live theatre in Squamish. We also performed in Brackendale, Britannia Beach, Woodfibre, Whistler and Pemberton. Nearly everyone had day jobs and some even did shift work. We all worked extremely hard, not only as actors but also as backstage hands, set designers, sound and lighting personnel.

Our Howe Sound Drama Club club ran for 35 years and put on 90 plays. After it closed in 2000, I thought about all these people—community members—who put in so much time and effort to provide live entertainment and felt that they needed to be honoured in some way. Four of us got together. We decided to gather memorabilia including programs, write-ups and photos of all those 90 plays and create a book. Since then, we have gathered about 2000 items for what we have termed the Howe Sound Drama Club Historical Project. (At the time of writing, the project is still in progress—still in need of funds to get the book printed!)

TEENAGE YEARS

Teenage Years

Teenage years suddenly came upon us. I felt shift work at the hospital was a poor choice at this juncture. A new office had just been built housing three new doctors. I applied to work from 9am to 5pm, and was accepted. Initially, when I saw a slack day at the clinic coming up, I did a casual shift at the hospital. I guess I hated giving it up entirely. But soon that became out of the question. The clinic thrived and became another part of the growing community.

It was good to be home at regular hours though many of my evenings were then taken up with rehearsals. Basically the kids were good. Helen was desperate to loosen the bonds that tied which I, never having wished that myself, never really caught on to. Eventually she succeeded and, though we didn't approve, it was the best way for her to learn life and what was most important. Helen always had a job, culminating in a lifetime of banking. Giving up her beloved horse was tough but—life goes on. Marriage, with two sons following, gave her much satisfaction.

After graduating, Bruce joined Up with People, a group teaching all forms of art including the technical aspects. They travelled the world, performing musical shows and staying with host families along the way. It was a great experience from which Bruce has never looked back.

Sarah went into management and has never looked back either.

Am I proud of my children? I couldn't be more so. We are a tight-knit family, which is an indescribable blessing. They have given me six wonderful, healthy grandchildren. Bruce is the only one settled out of Canada but we remain in close touch.

A Twist of Fate

Around 1980 I noticed a CBC advertisement in the *Vancouver Sun*—they were seeking actors and actresses. I quickly answered by handwritten letter (no emails back then) but heard nothing, until a year later, when I received a letter from CBC stating that they were updating their files. Was I still interested?

I replied immediately and was subsequently booked in for an audition. I got the part and was thrilled. I juggled my work at the clinic where everyone seemed as excited as I was. After my first movie experience was over, the girl whom I had shared a dressing room with, asked me who my agent was. I was dumbfounded. I had no idea what she was talking about. She explained and gave me the name of her agent, Morton Talent. I wrote them immediately and was accepted. Then I was on a roll.

First was *Beachcombers*, followed by small movies and commercials. Then came the big moment, an audition for a movie with Katharine Hepburn. I couldn't believe it when I was accepted. It was an experience of a lifetime as there were other great stars in this movie, *Mrs. Delafield Wants to Marry*. To mix with them and get to know them, their individual quirks and fantasies was truly amazing. Katherine was so totally with it and wouldn't allow any stand-ins while rehearsing. She was just one of us and delightful.

Another fun film was *The Big Year* with Steve Martin, Jack Black and Owen Wilson. I was also in Stephen King's *It* as well as *Scary Movie* and *The Best Christmas Pageant Ever* with Loretta Swit.

Although my movie career was the best paid, it was the least arduous. In *Scary Movie* I had two words to say—until the director corrected me and told me to "stand up, slash her throat and say, 'Your ass is grass.'" I was duly commended on such a line. How easy can that be?

One commercial was scary, as I had to be lowered by my back flat onto a parking lot of a Superstore. I was literally in the hands of the crew.

For another commercial, for Lotto 6/49, I had 30 minutes to learn to drive a moped in the BC Place parking lot. I then "won" my prize—a Harley Davidson—and was decked out in leathers, helmet and goggles.

My daughter, who was fond of bikers at the time, said, "Mom, we've gone full circle."

In *Diary of a Wimpy Kid: Rodrick Rules*, I sat on a toilet in the ladies' washroom while a small boy inched his way in under the door. I hit him with my handbag and called him a pervert. That was fun!

The last movie I did had many names but it was when my granddaughter came to say goodbye to me and she started to cry. Without a thought, tears welled up in my eyes and I did likewise. Never before or since have I wept "made-to-order" tears. I must have sensed my movie career was about to end.

Sadly, it came to a halt after I broke my back in 2014. I just couldn't drive to Vancouver for auditions anymore. However, on requesting my retirement from the actors' union, the ACTRA, I was advised that I could not retire as I was a life member! My many delightful roles in these forms of art had certainly been a wonderful experience as well as a good source of income and endless fun.

Ken

I sometimes called Ken a rough diamond. Our lives together were great. Ken was the most unselfish man. We realized that we both had the same values. He was generous to a fault, willing to help anyone who came his way. Living in Squamish was the best part of Ken's life, though he was never without pain. Working a crane proved agony for him so he applied for an accounting job at the mill. This was an improvement until the chemical plant offered him a job in their warehouse. He enjoyed it but eventually crossed swords with the assistant manager and was fired. What next?

Our bank manager suggested Ken apply for transporting the mail from Vancouver to Nelson. Ken loved driving so bid on the job and got it. First he had to buy a vehicle, then find a man who would share the job so that Ken could drive to Manning Park, exchange vehicles and mail with the man from Nelson and drive home. Ken was lucky to find such a responsible man. So off he would go around 1pm, drive to Vancouver, pick up mail from the post office and drive on, completing the exchange, drive back, getting home around 1am. A tiring job but he enjoyed it. He then found another man to spell him off one night a week.

After two years the job was up for bids again, but Ken lost out. What next?

A logger suggested to Ken that he should buy a Hiab truck and offer a pickup- and delivery service between Squamish and Vancouver. Ken bought a used Hiab and happily went to work for various companies. He transported the windows from Vancouver to the Rendezvous in Whistler, which entailed navigating twenty-one switchbacks to reach the appointed place halfway to the top of Blackcomb mountain.

During all these jobs, Ken was an avid member of the Squamish Lions Club. He helped run the volunteer ambulance before the province took over the ambulance service and was a volunteer paramedic. He helped raise money for the Easter Seals organization to create Camp Squamish for children with disabilities. On top of all this, he was a committed father to his children. He was stern, yet loving to them all. He allowed me to continue those things that were dear to me—nursing and acting. I was off rehearsing while he was coping with suppers and bedtime.

When I was on night duty at the hospital, Ken was there at home. The children had grown older when his night job took over. But he was always concerned about his three beloved children. Ken and I tried to work together as a team, discussing, trying to solve problems that beset us. (And there were many!)

After Ken's mother died in 1966, his father decided to come live with us. Ken's father was an avid photographer, retired from engineering but employed as a photographer by *National Geographic* magazine. He was a diabetic and, owing to heart problems, could not be insured to travel to BC by ship. He flew from Peru, stopping in Mexico City where he ran the length of the airport to catch his connection. This proved his health downturn. He lived with us for ten days.

Saying goodnight to his son that first night, Ken's father said, "I haven't been able to say that for many years." So sad.

Ken took his father to Vancouver General Hospital where he died peacefully. His sister came from England to visit us and asked if we had given her brother a proper Jewish funeral! I was dumbfounded and asked if Ken was a Jew. Ken's aunt replied at once, "All the Ramus family are Jews." Shell-shocked I asked Ken, who had been an active member of the Anglican Church, about his religion. Apparently only his father was Jewish which calmed me. Nowadays what on earth does it matter but, coming from an Anglican family, it mattered a lot to me.

Ken's father left us 10,000 dollars. We gave a thousand to each child and spent the rest on a trip to my family in England and my sister in New York state.

KEN AND MYSELF

In the late 1970s Ken heard, through the Lions Club, of a fund that was helping to bring Irish children from Belfast to Canada to show them a peaceful life instead of the violence experienced in Northern Ireland. The Squamish Lions Club was accepted as host families, so without much fuss we opened our home to Angela, aged 11, for six weeks.

What an eye opener. Angela's first words that night were, "It's awful quiet." She was a delight to have around. Years later she brought her Mam and stayed for three weeks. She is now married with four children and has never lost touch.

ANGELA, HER MOTHER MYSELF AND KEN

Ken and I spent some wonderful holidays together in Hawaii, Mexico, and Australia. On our last trip, on a freighter to Buenos Aires, Ken fell, gashing his head open. The stewardess did her best to stitch him up while he sat on his bunk bed. Staff were wonderful. The next morning we pulled into Fortaleza. From there a pilot boat was dispatched from which Ken and I were transported into the port, eventually landing in the hospital. We stayed there for three days. Ken was in a room where I slept on a couch. X-rays were taken and no obvious bones were broken. We were then transported to a hotel where we stayed until flights were arranged to take us on to Rio where our ship was at anchor, all this without extra cost to us.

The other passengers had written on our cabin door, "Welcome home Ken."

Gradually Ken's health began to fail. He lost his speech and kept falling. It was an agonizing time, eventually culminating in permanent nursing care. Still, he remained always cheerful and interested in the family. The Lions Club would take him to their meetings, which he enjoyed. He loved his food, and his vodka and cranberry juice at supper.

Two months before he died, Sarah brought two- month-old Mitchell to see him. In a flash his speech was there. "Mitchell, I am sorry I am not going to see you grow up." We all stood round his bed—floored. *We* were the ones unable to speak.

Ken died on December 12th, 1995. A life well lived, with always his family closest to his mind. He was a man with a positive attitude overcoming all the setbacks in his life with such courage. He will be, forever, missed by us all.

Granpa's Pancake Mix

1-1/2 cups flour
3 tbsp sugar
3 tsp baking powder
1/2 tsp salt
1/2 tsp vanilla
1 egg
milk to mix

Mix all ingredients.
Add milk till mixture drops from spoon. Best if lumpy.
Cook on hot surface, flipping once.

OUR LAST FARENELL.
AFTER 70 YEARS OF FREINDSHIP.

What's Next?

After Ken died I retired from everything—nursing, teaching prenatal, and drama. Life was to be lived. I hopped on a freighter to travel round the world in 2000. It was the trip of a lifetime, visiting so many ports, meeting many people of different creeds and cultures. I had my eyes opened to the war in the Pacific, which had never touched me. So much to take in and learn, plus the time to do just that. I continued those smaller freighter trips and even set sail on a tall ship, a large traditionally-rigged sailing vessel, from Barbados to Rome. I was able to meet up with several members of the Blyth family to return a prayer book belonging to George Blyth, our great uncle who in 1887 was appointed the fourth Bishop of Jerusalem. Bethlehem and Galilee were incredible. I have these glorious experiences to sit back and reminisce over.

I visited family in England and my beloved Andre in France. Over the years I had kept in touch with Andre, mostly through letters. The last time I saw him, in 2005, we reminisced over our love affair. I reminded him of what he had told me on one of our walks through English countryside.

"I want to give you a baby," Andre had said in his fractured English.

As we now walked in the garden in Courcelles, I told Andre how at the time I had thought, "How kind!" I loved children but where would Andre get this baby? Some orphanage I expected. The subject had been dropped, as I didn't think I could look after a baby just yet.

Andre now remarked, "Well I did, but I didn't know how."

After that visit we parted at the railway station in Gournay-en-Bray. Our final farewell said it all. We now keep in touch by phone, which means so much to both of us.

My Olympic Experience

The phone rang. It was October 2009, and preparations for the 2010 Winter Olympics in Vancouver and Whistler were in fully swing. "Doreen, I have five friends in Switzerland who want to experience the Olympics. Any chance you could give advice about accommodation in Squamish or Whistler—cheap?!"

After giving my cousin the usual information about local hotels and bed-and-breakfasts, I mentioned as an afterthought that I could accommodate five adults in my basement if they didn't mind second class.

That was it! How much would I charge? I really had no idea. Local accommodations were cashing in on all this opportunity, but I wanted my bid to be reasonable. I asked 600 dollars per person for 10 days of bed and breakfast. They jumped at it.

As February 2010 approached, apprehension set in. One double bed, one double futon and a camp cot, would this do? What about food? Croissants? Eggs? Bacon? Oh goodness, what do these people eat? Electricity: would my circuits be able to handle all this? Heat: would my basement be warm enough? Hot water: would it be adequate? After all, my basement had only one shower. Was I charging too much? *Panic!*

I prepared as best I could, and at last the day came for my Swiss guests to arrive. A homemade Swiss flag adorned my house. Their rented car appeared in my driveway and I greeted the four men and one woman in the best Swiss-German I knew. They settled into my second-class basement and came upstairs to join me in a drink before I served them a salmon supper. As we sat chatting and sipping, trying to make each other understand our respective lingo, I inquired as to where they lived in Switzerland.

"We don't live in Switzerland, we live in Germany. Yes, we are all Germans."

MY OLYMPIC EXPERIENCE

My heart sank. I had lived in England throughout the war years. For this then-teenager, bombing was an everyday experience during which hatred of all Germans had become rife. Worse still, my husband had been wounded at the front line and suffered from his wounds for the rest of his life. I remembered his angry quotes.

"The only good German is a dead one."

"No German is ever allowed to cross this threshold."

I felt the house shake and uttered a silent prayer, "Ken forgive me."

To my surprise and delight these five Germans were a pleasure to have in my home. They never complained, were up early, ate a full, good breakfast—I cooked a total of 100 eggs and 10 pounds of bacon, plus a variety of other goodies—and were then off to Whistler to ski or witness many of the competitions, or to Vancouver to explore and soak up the hype that was all so much part of the Games. We were able to discuss wars, political news and views. I was truly uplifted by their company.

Our final parting was sad. They all promised to return and bring their friends (HELP). Each of them left with a backdoor key.

What a lesson learned. Is there not enough hatred in this world without harping back as to what was? Surely this is what the Olympic movement is really about—understanding others and breaking down barriers. I feel honoured yet humbled by this experience and grateful to have been given the chance to redeem myself.

Though I regret being so far from my original family, my life in Canada has given me so much for which to be thankful. I keep in touch with the families in England and the US. They in turn fill me with all their news. Ken's family has overwhelmed me with love and acceptance into their vast numbers. I value this tremendously.

Because of Ken's war injuries, I am able to maintain my life in my house. His pension, garden and house maintenance enables me to live alone and welcome family plus so many friends when the spirit moves. Apart from a broken back, I am healthy. I keep my sense of humour uppermost. I am here to help my family and for me that is what counts because in the end they will be the ones to help me. At 90 years of age, I am the luckiest person alive.

My Kitchen

Clutter—most people would call it thus! I have lived in it for fifty-two years and love it. Appliances, some no longer used, abound. Fridge covered in mementos and piled high with useful "don't put away" valuables. Counters covered with "not sure where to put this just now" but a source of interest to many. Newspapers scattered on the table, crosswords uppermost! Comfort.

Cooking? Not my forte, but I have managed to feed and nurture my husband, three children, and many visitors without too many complaints. The phone rings, which brings news of overwhelming joy or devastating sadness. It is all absorbed and dealt with in those four walls.

So what is it about a kitchen? Is it the hub of family life? I often think so. Tears have fallen, advice given, discussions encouraged. Problems aired, sometimes solved, but always in the comfort of that cluttered room.

At one stage of my life I scrubbed the floor every night for a week, to prevent myself from madly tearing my hair out, waiting after midnight for my errant teenager to come home. We laugh about it now but the floor bore the brunt of my anger!

I hope my kitchen now can feel that it not only has fed the body with my questionable cooking but it has also fed many souls with love and understanding.

Look back and marvel at the guidance you have received and thank God.

Acknowledgements

I would like to acknowledge the enduring encouragement of Graham Fuller, Geraldine Guilfoyle, and Riun Blackwell. Without their enthusiasm, I may not have pressed forward with my writing.

I also would like to acknowledge Margreet Dietz for her editing expertise, for helping weave together more cohesively the anecdotes of my life and, in addition, for all of the production work involved in creating this book.

28663347R00097

Printed in Great Britain
by Amazon